Battle and Battle Description in Homer

Battle and Battle Description in Homer:

A Contribution to the History of War

Dr Franz Albracht

Translated and edited by
Peter Jones, Malcolm Willcock
and Gabriele Wright

Part I
*Supplement to the Annual Report of the Royal
State School Pforta, published at Naumburg on
the Saale, 1886, Programme Number 227*

Part II
*Supplement to the Annual Report of the Cathedral
Grammar School at Naumburg on the Saale,
1895, Programme Number 246*

Duckworth

First published in 2005 by
Gerald Duckworth & Co. Ltd.
90-93 Cowcross Street, London EC1M 6BF
Tel: 020 7490 7300
Fax: 020 7490 0080
inquiries@duckworth-publishers.co.uk
www.ducknet.co.uk

First published in German in
1886 and 1895 (see title page).

English translation © 2005 by Peter Jones,
Malcolm Willcock and Gabrielle Wright.
Preface © 2005 by Peter Jones
Appendix © 2005 by Malcolm Willcock.

A catalogue record for this book is available
from the British Library

ISBN 0 7156 3241 8

Typeset by Ray Davies
Printed and bound in Great Britain by
Biddles Ltd, King's Lynn, Norfolk

Contents

Foreword

Franz Albracht (1848-1909) was senior classical master at the presti-
gious Landesschule Pforta in eastern Germany from 1876 to 1892,
and then Headmaster of the nearby Domgymnasium at Naumburg
from 1892 till his death. As a young man he had served in the army
in the Franco-Prussian war of 1870-1, and his own personal experience of warfare permeates his discussion of the battle scenes in the
Iliad, just as he argues (p. 20) that the clarity and understanding of
Homer's descriptions show that Homer himself had had personal
experience in the field. Albracht was a distinguished Homeric scholar, one of the contributors to Ebeling's massive *Lexicon Homericum*
(1871-85). The two parts of his *Kampf und Kampfschilderung bei
Homer* appeared as appendixes to Annual Reports of the above
schools, the location of the publication of many scholarly papers in
nineteenth-century Germany.

We undertook the translation of *Kampf und Kampfschilderung bei
Homer* because we believe it to be still the best available account of
battle in Homer, written clearly and persuasively in straightforward,
non-technical language, with many ingenious solutions to a range of
problems. The latest writer on the subject, O. Hellmann, describes it
as 'the most comprehensive analysis of the battle descriptions to date'
(*Die Schlachtszenen der Ilias* [Stuttgart 2000], p. 14).

PJ was the leader of the team. He has written the Preface, sum-
marising and commenting on Albracht's work. MW, who proposed this
particular book for translation into English, has supplied the foot-
notes to the translation, the bibliography, index locorum and
Appendix. All Greek has been translated. For this purpose we have
used E.V. Rieu, *Homer: The Iliad* (revised by Peter Jones),
Harmondsworth 2003, and E.V. Rieu, *Homer: The Odyssey* (revised by
D.C.H. Rieu), Harmondsworth 1988, modified where necessary to suit
the precise point made by Albracht. Occasional inaccuracies in
Albracht's line or page references have been silently corrected.

The translation was done by GW, but all have contributed to it. PJ
must take responsibility for the final result.

January 2005   Peter Jones
                                                  Malcolm Willcock
                                                   Gabriele Wright

7

Conventions

1. References enclosed in square brackets are to the page numbers of Albracht's original text. These are marked in bold in the translation as e.g. **[I.23]**, **[II.7]**, where **I** refers to Part I (1886) and **II** to Part II (1895).

2. We have chosen to keep Albracht's traditional use of letters of the Greek alphabet to refer to the books of Homer. Capitals refer to the *Iliad*, minuscules to the *Odyssey*, thus:

Il.	Od.	Book
A	α	1
B	β	2
Γ	γ	3
Δ	δ	4
E	ε	5
Z	ζ	6
H	η	7
Θ	θ	8
I	ι	9
K	κ	10
Λ	λ	11
M	μ	12
N	ν	13
Ξ	ξ	14
O	ο	15
Π	π	16
P	ρ	17
Σ	σ	18
T	τ	19
Y	υ	20
Φ	φ	21
X	χ	22
Ψ	ψ	23
Ω	ω	24

Preface

Peter Jones

Albracht begins by assuming that Homer's battle scenes, while primarily a poetic construct, reflect a basic historical reality. He admits that drawing lines between the one and the other is extremely difficult but is sympathetic to the view that Homer himself observed and fought in battles [I.3-4].[1]

At [I.5-13] Albracht deals with preparations for battle. Understanding that the army was perceived not as a single unit, but a collection of privately trained tribes and families, he sees that the overall leader, Agamemnon, can have no ultimate authority over these individual contingents under the control of their personal leaders like Diomedes, Ajax and Nestor.[2] Strategy and tactics therefore go out of the window. Battle, once started, goes on till it stops, without any possibility of overall control or intervention. All the leader and his senior advisory council can do, therefore, is to make sure the army is drawn up properly before launching it into action [I.6-7]. So the basic sequence goes (with food, sacrifices, exhortations etc. thrown in *ad lib.*): order for battle; arming; the men move to the meeting place; there they are sorted and drawn up; the advance [I.8-9]. It is a lengthy business, beginning early in the morning, and there is a skill involved in drawing up the troops efficiently. There is also an especial emphasis on the *promachoi* 'front-line fighters', leaders and heroes who set an example to the rest by their individual prowess [I.10].

The depth of the formation and its cohesiveness are a matter of guesswork, though Albracht speculates that it must have been fairly loosely formed to allow warriors to brandish and throw spears; he rejects the idea that the *gephurai* of battle, literally 'bridges', are longitudinal gaps between the front and subsequent lines, wide enough for chariots to pass along [I.11-12]. He agrees that ranks could be tightly formed to start with, but argues that a looser formation would inevitably develop as they marched into battle.

At [I.13-24] Albracht digresses on the use of chariots. Pointing out that they are never used in massed formation (except in a tale of his youth placed in old Nestor's mouth, [I.14]), he goes on to argue that, since they are manned by heavily armed foot-soldiers who fight as such, their purpose is not martial; they are used first and foremost as a platform for advance and retreat [I.16]. He firmly rejects the idea

9

that they might form the front rank of the army [I.17]. Albracht then examines and interprets a number of passages to illustrate how the chariots are used in battle and relate to the activities of the rest of the troops, whether advancing or retreating, especially Books 5, 8, 11 and 16 [I.17-20]. He also discusses their use as an 'ambulance' and the skills required by the drivers, especially holding the chariot in position close to the fighter; the dangers inherent in the driver's position are emphasised [I.20-2]. Throughout, Albracht offers clever solutions to and radical interpretations of a range of problems.

[I.24-7] deal with the advance into battle. Albracht, making the point that there is no sign of any unified 'signal for the advance', sees this too as a matter for individual commanders to decide, who take their contingents into battle as they see fit. He also sees the distinction between Greek silence and Trojan hubbub as a feature not of the moment of advance into battle itself (which would be characterised by battle-cries on both sides) but of the preceding sequence, as they move from the mustering-place towards the battle area. Albracht interprets the Greek silence as a precursor of the disciplined Dorian advance [I.25-6]. The heroes are always in the front line; some of them step out in advance of it to act as an example and start the engagement.

At [I.27-34] Albracht turns to the (controversial) 'standing fight'. He understands this as a time when the battle lines are essentially stationary, and combat is engaged between individuals or small groups in the space between the two enemy front lines.[3] He contrasts it with the massed assault, designed to break the enemy lines and turn them in flight – which, he maintains, is the real purpose of the battle.[4] Essentially, he sees battle as veering between these two styles in the following sort of sequence: standing fight – massed assault – retreat or rout – lines regroup – standing fight, etc. [I.27].

Albracht also observes that, whereas most of the fighting is of the 'single combat' type, Homer now and again refers to both armies engaging on a massive scale, and to the field being littered with dead. As a result, he suggests that the 'single-combat' style of fighting is simply meant as an example of what is happening all along the line, designed to illustrate the whole course of battle at that moment [I.28]. Albracht now illustrates this thesis with a series of examples and, using Idomeneus as his main model, draws particular attention to the need of the warrior not only to be a skilful fighter but also to show agility and quickness of foot as he darts in to strip an enemy and darts back again, and as he ducks and dodges enemy spears [I.31-2].

Albracht covers the second type of fighting, massed attack to break through the opposing line, at [I.34-40]; and finds it quite credible that the assault of a single warrior could create the circumstances from which such a breakthrough could occur. For it to be successful, however, the men must be drawn up in a tight, closed formation. A similar formation is needed if such an attack is to be successfully defended [I.34-6], and Albracht spends some time convincingly explaining the 'overlapping spears' of the Greek defensive formation in Book 13 [I.36-8]. He draws a telling contrast between the massed formations struggling over the body of Patroclus in Book 17 and the comparatively relaxed 'standing fight' going on in another part of the field [I.39-40]; and distinguishes between the 'spears raised' and 'spears lowered' positions, whose adoption by a massed force depended on particular circumstances.

The end-game of any encounter is the flight and pursuit of the enemy. Albracht turns to this at [I.41-52]. He begins by pointing out that a more or less controlled retreat is a preferable option to flight, and that the epic distinguishes between a massed, fighting retreat and an organised rearguard action, in which a small group covers the retreat of the rest of the army [I.41-2]. The flight or rout, however, is a major disaster. The pursuers can slaughter at will an enemy with its back turned, as long as they have the stamina. Albracht sees two particular features of Homer's description of this event: first, the use of the chariot, whose speed makes it the best means of both flight and pursuit; and second, the bloody consequences for the routed – they alone are killed in these encounters. Whereas, in retreat, the lines are maintained, in rout they break up very quickly, all the more because those with chariots – the best heroes – get away at speed, leaving the slower foot-soldiers even more unprotected. Often it takes the intervention of a god to halt a rout.

At the same time, the lines of the pursuing enemy also would loosen, and if those in flight did manage to rally, the enemy also would have to do so in order to mount a defence. As a result, a fleeing enemy could sometimes retrieve a difficult situation quite successfully [I.42-3]. An example of the rout in Book 5 is described, with a detailed discussion of a particular problem at 5.505-6 when the Trojans rally and the Greek charioteers (who would be ahead of the foot-soldiers in the pursuit) turn back to rejoin the Greek lines [I.44-6]; Albracht notes how the temptation for the pursuers to stop and retrieve booty holds up the effectiveness of their onslaught. The routs in Books 8 and 11 are then analysed, the sudden and total reversal of fortune on the Greek side after the wounding of Agamemnon in Book 11 being brought about by Zeus. Patroclus' rout of the Trojans in Book 16 is discussed [I.46-50]. Further examples are given from Books 17 and 20-1. Albracht comments that it is typical for a single hero to hold up a rout for a time, and it is a sign of the absolute panic Achilles induces in Books 20-1 that no Trojan attempts to do this [I.50-1]; finally, he moves on to examine passages where heroes attempt to hold up a rout

11

on foot (far more dangerous than in a chariot), e.g. Odysseus in Book 11 [I.51-2].

The introduction to Part II of Albracht's book, published nine years later, reiterates the views advanced in [I.3-4] about Homer's 'poeticisation' of what must have been understood by his audience as some of the basic realities of war [II.1-3].

At [II.3-8] Albracht discusses how the besieging Greek army protected itself from Trojan attack. This was important. The only quarters the Greeks have are their *klisiai* 'huts' (literally 'lean-tos') by their ships, where they have been living for ten years. They need to defend them, and the wall proposed by Nestor in Book 7 is designed for that purpose (in the 'real' world, of course, the wall would have been built on their arrival, as Thucydides remarks). Albracht argues that the 'towers' in the walls refer essentially to protective enlargements on either side of the gates, designed to hold a good number of soldiers on the upper level to defend them in the case of attack (the gates being the most vulnerable points in the walls). The accompanying ditch is not dug right next to the wall, but some way from it, and can be negotiated by chariots only slowly and with great care; as a result, crossing-places are built into the ditch, opposite the gates. The 'stakes' set up along the ditch on the Greek side are obviously omitted at the crossing-places [II.3-6]. Albracht finds the (probably non-Homeric) Book 10 wholly in agreement with good military practice. The Greeks are in danger; the wall has therefore been built and guards posted (note the especial emphasis on the guards at the crossing places). It is the most natural thing in the world to inspect these guards, as it is indeed to send spies by night to the enemy camp [II.6-7]. Albracht takes it as a mark of Trojan incompetence that they do not have an efficient system of guards when they sleep out on the plain [II.8].

Albracht devotes the next chapter [II.9-15] to the way such a fortified camp is attacked and defended. He distinguishes two types of attack. In Book 12, it is carried out without chariots, since Hector agrees with Polydamas that, while the chariots might, with suitable care and caution, cross the ditch and move towards the Greek camp, they could never re-cross it at speed if the Greeks successfully counter-attack. The forces therefore split into five contingents of foot-soldiers, three of which are described as they attack the gates and wall at separate points. Albracht notes that scaling ladders are not used – the aim is to force an entry – and emphasises the lowness of the wall. Sarpedon tears down a stretch of defensive breastwork and the two sides face each other over the wall; Hector smashes down the main gate and the Trojans pour through that as well as over the now undefended wall [II.9-13].

In Book 15, Albracht sees a different type of attack, this time along the whole length of the wall by the whole Trojan army, acting as one, chariots and all. It is greatly facilitated by Apollo, who fills in the ditch and knocks down part of the wall. Albracht sees no inconsistency in the chaos which the ditch causes the Trojans when Patroclus drives them out of the camp in Book 16: Apollo, he argues, had only roughly filled it in [II.13-15].

Finally, Albracht turns to the siege and defence of a fortified city [II.15-25]. His crucial observation here is that, while many other types of combat are described in the *Iliad*, the strategies, methods of assault or even most basic requirements for capturing a well-fortified town like Ilium receive no mention of any sort whatsoever. At the same time, the *Iliad* constantly refers to the capture and sacking of other cities in the course of raids for booty, e.g. Thebe. Presumably the reason is that they are not defended with anything like the walls of Ilium; but at the same time the characters are constantly expressing the hope that Ilium's capture and sacking will eventually be achieved [II.15-17].

Yet there are no references to e.g. cutting off access to water[5] or interrupting supplies. The only means of taking Ilium, in fact, seems to be defeating the Trojan army in open battle on the plain. The Curetes' bombardment of the city of Calydon described by Phoenix in Book 9 is the nearest Homer comes to describing anything like an assault by a besieging army, though the possibility of scaling the walls is advanced in a few places. In other words, the art of siege is not known.[6] At the same time, the ultimate fate of a besieged city is regularly described – destruction by fire [II.17-19].

Albracht now goes on to discuss the 'towers' built into the walls of Ilium and their defensive uses, and compares them with (what were for him the recent) archaeological finds at Hissarlik; again he emphasises that, even when the Greeks approach the walls and towers, all they do is slope their shields on their shoulders, as if that is the limit of their tactics when they are up against the walls of the town. Even when Andromache suggests Hector should retreat, she does not propose that he fight from inside the walls, but just outside the walls 'by the fig-tree'. But that he cannot do. Heroic action requires that he fight in the forefront of the action on the plain. Albracht concludes that the besiegers are there to invite the besieged to fight. It is up to the Trojans, in other words, to drive the Greeks away; otherwise, it is stalemate [II.20-2].[7]

As far as the Trojans are concerned, it is clear that the Greeks will never take Ilium by any other means than defeating them in open field. Given the deprivations they and their allies suffer, however, they have no option but to try to drive the Greeks away (though

Homer does briefly raise the possibility of the Trojans buying them off). Homer gives no indication that the Greeks attempt to cut Ilium off from the outside world (cf. the ease with which Priam makes his journey to Achilles in Book 24). Indeed, when Ilium does finally fall, it falls to a *trick* – so impotent is the Greek army in the face of the city with its lovely walls and its heroic Trojan defenders [II.22-5].[8]

Notes

1. With our post-Parryan understanding of the way the oral poet worked, we might wish to resist this conclusion and argue instead that the battle scenes owe very little to the poet's experience of war and much more to his experience as an oral poet, drawing on a tradition of oral story-telling steeped in stories of battle and going back hundreds of years. In other words, the tradition provided Homer with the means of producing battle scenes in the epic manner, whether true to life or not. Given, therefore, such rich story-telling resources, there was no need for the poet to have engaged in or witnessed battles personally for him to be able to describe them in the approved epic way.

In fact, there is much good sense in what Albracht says about the extent to which Homer represents an experience of battle which his listeners would understand, in two particular respects: first, the nature of hand-to-hand fighting itself and, second, the value system such fighting generates (it is worth mentioning that Albracht himself fought in battle: see Foreword). In *Apocalypse* (Tempus 2002) 242-6, Neil Faulkner describes in Homeric terms the fighting between Jewish and Roman soldiers at the Temple Mount in AD 70, and draws parallels with Agincourt, citing John Keegan, *The Face of Battle* (Harmondsworth 1978): ' "as movement died out of the two hosts [at Agincourt], we can visualise them divided, at a distance of ten or fifteen feet, by a horizontal fence of waving and stabbing spear shafts, the noise of their clattering like that of a bully-off at hockey magnified several hundred times" [Keegan]. There is, in fact, an almost overpowering "terror of cold steel", which ensures that a line which does not flinch in the face of an enemy charge is almost guaranteed to bring the enemy to a halt immediately in front of it. ... What men feared when they contemplated crossing the last few yards to close fully with the enemy was not just death or injury, but steel slicing through flesh, agonising and horrific wounds, the possibility of mutilation and permanent disablement.' This style of 'stand off' matches almost exactly the situation Homer describes in the *stadiê makhê* 'standing fight', the most common type of engagement (see p. 53).

Faulkner then goes on to discuss the military values that such a style of engagement generates, and quotes General Marshall's study of American soldiers in the Second World War: 'Whenever one surveys the forces of the battlefield, it is to see that fear is general among men, but to observe further that men are commonly loath that their fear will be expressed in specific acts which their comrades will recognise as cowardice. The majority are unwilling to take extraordinary risks and do not aspire to a hero's role, but they are equally unwilling that they should be considered the least worthy among those present. ... When a soldier is ... known to the men who are round him, he ... has reason to fear losing the one thing he is likely to value more highly than life – his reputation as a man among other men.' The 'glorious reputation' that Homeric heroes seek in battle, then, is not a Homeric invention but grounded in the conditions of hand-to-hand engagement with which every member of Homer's audience would have been fully acquainted.

2. Albracht talks of 'princes' and 'kings' throughout his monographs. This image of royalty at war is misleading. These days we tend to talk more neutrally of 'leaders'.

3. See n. 1.

4. For the debate over phalanxes and massed assaults, see p. 139 and cf. V.D. Hanson (ed.), *Hoplites: the Greek Battle Experience* (Routledge 1991), 63-84.

5. The latest excavations have revealed extensive springs under the town itself.

6. We might prefer to say that a siege, even if it was known, does not offer a context for heroic glory that fighting on the plain, hand-to-hand against other heroes, does. Compare the constricted, 'unheroic' nature of the battles between Greeks and Trojans in the attack on the wall in Book 12. So the Trojans 'cannot' hunker down defensively behind their walls, nor the Greeks hang about outside cutting off water supplies, etc. That is not the stuff of epic.

7. Cf. P.V. Jones, 'Poetic invention: The Fighting around Troy in the First Nine Years of the Trojan War', in Ø. Andersen and M.W. Dickie (eds), *Homer's World: Fiction, Tradition, Reality* (Papers from the Norwegian Institute at Athens, vol. iii), 1995, 101-11.

8. Not to mention the will of the traditional epic poet.

Part I

Introduction

[I.1] In the following work I aim to give a comprehensive description, from a tactical point of view, of the battles and engagements in the heroic age on the basis of their description in the books of Homer. Though this does not produce new results at every point, it may still perhaps hope to be regarded as a new contribution to the history of war, since it seeks to build up a general picture out of details viewed at times from a standpoint different from that normally taken, and to make it possible to survey the state of military practice in the heroic age. It will perhaps also be welcome to a wider circle of friends and interpreters of the poet if its narrowly-focused examination succeeds in throwing a different and, as I hope, a more accurate light on some passages of the epic; or if it merely succeeds in stimulating us to examine again some of the questions we encounter in this area with more precision than has been applied to them up to now, in some cases repeatedly. For Homer has always been regarded as the 'staff handbook' on heroic tactics, in which the sum total of military knowledge of the Greek heroic age has been set down; from which one can derive not only historical knowledge, but also knowledge which could be put to good use on a tactical level; so everyone who was interested in the history of warfare naturally resorted to the oldest written record on the subject, the poems of Homer (cf. Köpke, *Über das Kriegswesen der Griechen im heroischen Zeitalter*, Introduction). But the interpretation of the tactics which we encounter in the *Iliad* has, I think, been mistaken in some important respects. Köpke, who dealt with this question first and in most detail, on the one hand goes a great deal too far concerning, for example, the use of chariot fighters, but on the other, in his presentation of tactics in the heroic age (p. 215ff.), he does not do justice to the information already available. Friedreich, *Die Realien in der Iliade und Odyssee*, follows Köpke's interpretation precisely and frequently verbatim, without naming him; and the brief, summary overview of the history of Greek warfare by Köchly and Rüstow (pp. 1-7) contains many details which do not square with what is described in the epic. The excellent essay by Jähns, *Die Entwickelung des altgriechischen Kriegswesens*, Grenzboten 1878, deliberately deals only very briefly with this earliest period; and I do not think that the question at issue has in any way been answered or substantially advanced by the most recent

17

investigations of Buchholz in the second volume of his *Realien* (p. 303ff.), if we make the text of the epic the basis of our consideration.

So far it is the question of the arms and armour of the heroic age which has been most carefully and precisely investigated; apart from the works referred to above, I also mention: Hopf, *Das Kriegswesen im heroischen Zeitalter nach Homer*, Programm von Hamm 1847 and 1858. I can omit it completely from my enquiry since, especially after **[I.2]** the excellent work of Helbig, *Das homerische Epos aus den Denkmälern erläutert*, I must regard it as settled. But as to the results of these investigations of equipment, Jähns, op. cit., summarises as follows: 'Thus in terms of tactics and siege warfare, the battle round Ilium still gives a very primitive picture, which differs greatly from the more advanced stages of development of the Greek art of warfare; on the other hand, curiously enough, the essential weaponry which was to be of importance in the following period is already fixed in this early age – apart from the late Hellenic artillery'. It is precisely this conclusion which seems to me to give cause for some reservations. For advances in weapons and armour cannot, I think, be so completely divorced from advances in their use. Rather, they go hand in hand at all times, depend on each other or follow each other within short periods of time. The epic itself also gives expression to the opinion that there is a close connection between weapons and method of fighting, when it reports that the Locrians are not yet armed with shield and spear, but only with the bow, N 712-22, and for this reason they are not suited to the σταδίη μάχη 'standing fight'.[1] The Locrians hold the old attitude which did not envisage the possibility of real fighting between concentrations of troops, so they fight, as their weapons demand, only from a distance. Now if at the same time we find the other tribes by and large (though not uniformly) armed with helmet, shield, breastplate, greaves, sword and spear – as in the more developed tactics of the later period – then there is from the start a definite probability in the view that already in the Homeric age it is possible to find at least the beginnings of an art of war which actually allowed for the heavy arming of the ordinary troops and not just of individual outstanding leaders and heroes, and thus the use of massed troops in battle.

Furthermore, the battles which the epic describes for us are no longer being fought primarily for the prize of heroic virtue and bravery, but for victory – which (apart from honour and glory) also restores peace and quiet. The period in which the heroic songs of the *Iliad* were sung demonstrates a striking cultural development; an important epoch of war had preceded it which had led to the perfection of weaponry and at the same time to value being placed on an organised method of fighting and the deployment of the masses as a fighting force. Since for Homeric heroes the fight is no longer an end in itself, but essentially a means to an end, and is frequently thought of as downright laborious (cf. Helbig, op. cit., pp. 294-5, Duncker, *Geschichte des Altertums* III p. 270), since they no longer derive pleasure from simply attacking and killing their opponent, since we encounter them in a war which has been planned for a long time, carefully prepared and waged in a far away country, since they have already learnt to appreciate the value of a finer civilisation and a higher culture, and since the mere desire for rich booty is no longer the motive for war, they must therefore have already begun to think of ways to force a quick win, to have in mind a more elaborate kind of warfare using highly developed weapons and exploiting numerical superiority. And I hope that a more precise examination of the battle scenes described in the epic will show that they are based on a by no means inconsiderable amount of tactical knowledge and skill.

In our investigation we must not, of course, disregard the fact that Homer is not a military author but a poet, that his purpose is not to sing of the art of contemporary warfare but the heroic exploits of his people, that he does not set out tactical principles in order to justify or explain the military dispositions that have been made or the orders that have been given, but at most weaves them into his descriptions to heighten their clarity and vividness **[I.3]** and because he and his listeners derive pleasure from them. All the same, Homer does construct his poetic creation on foundations based on reality; the military situations described by him, although embellished and decorated by the poet's imagination, have their basis in real life; the enthralling vividness, the graphic three-dimensionality of most of his battle scenes are not the product of mere poetic invention, but are based on practical experience, real observation. Even though in questions of art, and especially of architecture, one may have doubts whether the details of epic are taken from the real world in which the poet was living, or whether the bard had created for himself an ideal world, ideal surroundings and ideal art treasures for his poetic work, in the eminently practical question of warfare we stand on real ground. The principles of tactics, the advances in the difficult art of commanding and leading armies, were never derived from the imagination of poets or prophetically conceived by bards, but were achieved with blood and sweat step by step, in serious conflict, born from practical experience. So if we find traces of such tactical knowledge in the epic, if the poet presents us with a 'phalanx' in close order as an example to please even the God of War, and if he puts a shrewd tactical proposal in the mouth of now one, now another, leader proven in counsel and grown grey in battle, then we may use such features to construct for ourselves a picture of the understanding of the art of war at the time when the epic originated. Just as in the brilliant similes of the epic, taken from nature and human life, which we can, so to speak, verify for ourselves, we find vivid, sharp observation and faithful representation of even the smallest details which often make the picture particularly sharp, just as the poet everywhere we follow him surprises us and fills us with admiration for his sensitive observation and portrayal of behaviour arising from the psychology of the individual, so also his descriptions of battle scenes and the world of war arose from sharp and careful observation of real conditions.

In all this one has, of course, appropriately to allow wide scope to the imagination of the poet, who in his lay celebrates the martial glory of his ancestors; and in order to gain the most faithful picture of that time, the important thing is to determine the boundary where reality ends and the poet's imagination begins. It will not be possible to reach general agreement on where this line should exactly be drawn, but there are still quite a few individual features which can be described as indubitably taken from real life; and one will generally regard the regular or frequent recurrence of certain phenomena under similar circumstances as a criterion of reality. We intend to use these features to draw our picture of the tactical knowledge and practices of the heroic age. In doing so, it will not be possible to go into the different time of origin of individual passages of the epic; the possible results of our investigation are not sufficient for that. I also beg leave to refer to 'the poet' throughout, naturally without thereby passing judgement on this question or wanting to attribute all passages to one author.[2]

Finally, I regard it as superfluous to sing the praise of the poet's skill in battle descriptions, which is above all praise; in this area, too, they show him to us as a connoisseur of life and a master of description. As Frölich at the end of his book *Die Militärmedizin Homer's*, Stuttgart 1879, expresses the thought that Homer's unusual knowledge in this field makes it probable that the author of the *Iliad* had acquired it from practice and had been an army surgeon (so far as such existed at his time), and as Helbig concludes his investigation into the description of the Shield with **[I.4]** the words: 'if the poet had lived in an age of more advanced art, he would perhaps have become a great artist, and his name would have been spoken of alongside that of Polygnotus or Phidias'; so, in the same way, a more precise examination of the battle descriptions undoubtedly leads to the conviction that the poet had not merely observed battles and engagements and understood them, but had actually experienced them himself and fought in them. We gain this conviction, even if we approach our question with greater rationality and calm than the poet's enthusiastic admirer, Plato's Ion, who thought, 541 B, that ὅστις γε ἀγαθὸς ῥαψῳδός, καὶ στρατηγὸς ἀγαθός 'a good rhapsode is also a good general', and who, when Socrates asked ἢ καὶ στρατηγός, ὦ Ἴων, τῶν Ἑλλήνων ἄριστος εἶ; 'Are you then, Ion, the best general of the Greeks?' answered εὖ ἴσθι, ... καὶ ταῦτά γε ἐκ τῶν Ὁμήρου μαθών; 'Certainly, ... and I learnt it from Homer'; and even without following Napoleon (who was certainly competent to judge military questions), of whom Sainte-Beuve cites the following characteristic utterance (in 'Le premier livre de l'*Énéide*', *Revue Contemporaine*, Tome XXVIII 1856, p. 338): 'Quand on lit l'*Iliade*, on sent à chaque instant qu' Homère a fait la guerre, et n'a pas comme le disent les commentateurs passé sa vie dans les écoles de Chio ... Le journal d'Agamemnon ne serait pas plus exact pour les distances et le temps, et pour la vraisemblance des opérations militaires, que ne l'est son poème', 'When one reads the *Iliad*, one senses all the time that Homer had fought in battle and had not, as commentators claim, passed his life in the schools on Chios[3] ... Agamemnon's diary would not be more precise about distances and times and the record of military operations than is his poem.' Paul-Louis Courier in a letter to Villoison of 8 March 1805 even said (Sainte-Beuve, loc. cit.): 'Homère fit la guerre, gardez-vous d'en douter. C'était la guerre sauvage. Il fut aide-de-camp, je crois, d'Agamemnon, ou bien son secrétaire', 'Homer fought in battle, don't you doubt it. It was fierce fighting. He was Agamemnon's aide-de-camp, I believe, or else his secretary.'

In the discussion on which we now embark, I will keep to the order in which the successive events of a day of battle would probably follow one another. I will deal first, briefly, with the βουλή 'council', then the marshalling of the army, with an excursus on the use of chariots, then the advance, the 'standing fight', the massed battle, and finally, flight and pursuit.

[I.5] Council of War. Marshalling of the Army

An assembly of the leaders precedes all the more important military operations. Since the commander in chief had limited authority in relation to the other leaders, each of whom was free to make his own decisions, even during periods of the greatest danger and pressure, discussion and agreement were absolutely necessary for the whole army to act as one. If a battle was to be fought, the least one had to agree on was the order in which the individual tribes were to be deployed in relation to each other. Therefore the βουλή 'council' plays an important role in the episodes of war which the epic presents to us.

Another reason which makes some prior battle-planning appear necessary arises from the kind of fighting with which we are faced in the epic. For every encounter, the entire force which is available moves into battle; there is no mention of reserves, troops which would somehow be available for the commander in chief to be able to intervene in the course of the battle here or there; and it appears impossible to break off a battle once it has begun. Therefore, once it has been set in motion, the whole war-machine goes its way irrevocably until success has been achieved, or the army has been beaten back, or night prohibits any further fighting. Once battle has started, no repositioning of individual contingents occurs within the total mass. For that reason it is all the more important to fix their order beforehand, for which the βουλή 'council' offered the best opportunity. It usually took place in the tent and under the chairmanship of the commander in chief (when Achilles Ω 651 says that the Achaeans came to him for a conference every evening οἵ τέ μοι αἰεὶ βουλὰς βουλεύουσι παρήμενοι, ἧ θέμις ἐστίν 'they always come here to discuss tactics with me – it is our custom', one could envisage lower-level deliberations, just between the Myrmidon leaders); and it took place normally the evening before the battle, since preparations for drawing up the army had to begin early next morning. Therefore a βουληφόρος ἀνήρ, ᾧ λαοί τ' ἐπιτετράφαται καὶ τόσσα μέμηλεν 'a member of the council, who has an army in his charge, a man with much on his mind,' ought not to sleep through the whole night, B 24, 61. Even though the first pre-battle council which the epic mentions takes place in the morning, B 53ff., this has its natural cause in the special conditions assumed by the poet. In I 89ff., we find the *gerontes* 'elders' assembled in Agamemnon's tent in the evening in a group discussion over a meal (see Ameis' note on line 70). One should not take the notion of the participating γέροντες 'elders' too narrowly, and should surely take it to include all the independent leaders; for in the *Doloneia* the youthful Diomedes naturally belongs among them. In K 195 it is the Ἀργείων βασιλῆες 'Greek kings' with the sentry-commanders Meriones and Thrasymedes co-opted, who form the war council. Diomedes Ξ 112ff. affirms that it is not only age which matters, but also noble birth. Hector too summons to his war council (K 300) πάντας ἀρίστους, ὅσσοι ἔσαν Τρώων ἡγήτορες ἠδὲ μέδοντες 'all the leading men, the captains and councillors of the Trojans' and they constitute the βουληφόροι ἄνδρες 'members of the council', K 414.

Once the war council has decided in favour of battle, engagement must be preceded by the important and time-consuming business of marshalling the army. It goes without saying that **[I.6]** conditions applied if great numbers of men were to be used in the battle – and certainly they had been enrolled by their leaders for this purpose, something which Hector specifically says in P 221ff.:

οὐ γὰρ ἐγὼ πληθὺν διζήμενος οὐδὲ χατίζων
ἐνθάδ᾽ ἀφ᾽ ὑμετέρων πολίων ἤγειρα ἕκαστον,
ἀλλ᾽ ἵνα μοι Τρώων ἀλόχους καὶ νήπια τέκνα
προφρονέως ῥύοισθε φιλοπτολέμων ὑπ᾽ Ἀχαιῶν

'I neither sought nor needed mere numbers when I summoned each of you here from your own towns. What I wanted was men who would be fully committed to fighting the war-loving Greeks in defence of the women and little children of Troy'.

In these conditions, the battle had to be preceded by a reasonably well-ordered drawing-up of contingents, both individually and as units within the complete army (cf. also Köchly and Rüstow, *Kriegswesen*, p. 4). The importance and necessity of this consequently find full appreciation and confirmation in the epic, because not only are we given a detailed description of it before the first battle-day, but the drawing-up of both armies is expressly mentioned before almost every battle. To get to know it, let us follow the detailed presentation which the epic gives us before the start of the first battle, B 441ff.

It is preceded by an assembly of the whole unarmed army in the camp, in which the leaders' decision to fight is announced. In this assembly, B 362, Nestor advises Agamemnon – and here the poet gives the first example of a technique which he often employs, that of putting important tactical rules or principles in the mouth of an old and experienced army leader – κρῖν᾽ ἄνδρας κατὰ φῦλα, κατὰ φρήτρας, Ἀγάμεμνον 'Sort your men out, Agamemnon, into their tribes and clans'. This proposal by the venerable Pylian, in spite of the praise of it by Agamemnon in 370ff., should not of course be regarded as an innovation introduced by Nestor now for the first time in the tenth year of the war, by which he wished to suggest to the commander in chief an idea wholly unknown until then; instead, it confirms the natural principle of organisation of an army made up of different tribes, corresponding to the political conditions of the poet's time and to the situation assumed by him. For epic does not yet know an army as a unit, obedient to a single command, but only as a collection of tribes which have united for common action in war; it does not yet know of differently armed groups which, detached from their tribal connections, could go into action as tactical units. Consequently, and contrary to opinions which are often expressed, it does not yet know of mounted troops, squadrons of chariot fighters which could be drawn up and deployed by Agamemnon as a tactical force now here, now there, depending on the conditions of the terrain or the battle. It knows even less of any real joint operation of different sections of the army under a higher command. As a result, there is not yet a single tactical principle governing the structure of the entire army, but it is rather a matter of each tribe being drawn up for battle around its leader or leaders. Compare, for example, Δ 90 εὖρε Λυκάονος υἱὸν ... ἀμφὶ δέ μιν κρατεραὶ στίχες ἀσπιστάων λαῶν, οἵ οἱ ἕποντο 'she found the son of Lycaon ... and around him the powerful shield-bearing force that had come under his command', and similarly 201, 295, 328, 330, Λ 57-60 and numerous other passages; and when in Υ 2 it says θωρήσσοντο ἀμφὶ σέ, Πηλέος υἱέ, μάχης ἀκόρητον 'Αχαιοί 'the Greeks armed for battle, led by you, son of Peleus, always spoiling for a fight', this expression merely takes account of the high profile Achilles enjoys at this point in the story.

So the tribes constitute the only divisions of the army, and within the φῦλα 'tribes', family groups form the subdivisions. We should not be surprised that this principle is expressed so precisely only once. It was simply a matter of course, and is a premise underlying all descriptions of battle and war. Indeed, to a limited extent, it still remained valid for the following period of development of Greek tactics, cf. Köchly and Rüstow, op. cit., Section B, up to the battle of Plataea, p. 45: 'The organisation by local groups, clans or other tribal and community units determined the line-up of the **[I.7]** battle-front within the contingent of one and the same people, of one and the same state. If a Greek army consisted of the contingents of several states, then these state contingents constituted the larger units of the whole and closed up together from the right wing to the left.' Rüstow, *Heerwesen und Kriegsführung Cäsars*, p. 24, says of the Roman auxiliary troops: 'One may assume that, with short-term levies which did not stay together long, the arrangement of the contingents was merely based on the communities and areas from which they were sent' (cf. also Jähns, op. cit., p. 6). Again, the reasoning which the poet puts in Nestor's mouth corresponds to the picture which we should have of the training of an army in heroic times: 'The men' (he argues) 'will be more inclined to support each other within their clans', Β 363. Since they are fighting in units of compatriots, κατὰ σφέας γὰρ μαχέονται 366, 'each man will be fighting at his brother's side', 'you will all the better be able to judge the quality of the leaders in the behaviour of their men and vice versa', 365. For the commander always leads only his own compatriots and is thus, so to speak, responsible for their performance; there are no combined training exercises; the young hero is trained in the use of weapons from his youth; he brings his own people to war and battle; and it is his task to train them through practice. During a war as long as the siege of Troy, this could very well be managed through individual raids and campaigns, which the leaders frequently undertook on their own initiative. The Myrmidons are the best among the Achaeans because their leader is the most able, Ρ 165 ἀνέρος, i.e. of Achilles, ὃς μέγ' ἄριστος 'Αργείων ... καὶ ἀγχέμαχοι

Part I

θεράποντες 'who is the best warrior in the Greek camp, with the best men at close combat under his command'. Moreover, who is better able than the local king, or the leaders appointed by him, to identify any cowards during the marshalling, who have lagged behind in spite of the severe punishment for this offence pronounced by the supreme commander, B 391-3

ὃν δέ κ' ἐγὼν ἀπάνευθε μάχης ἐθέλοντα νοήσω
μιμνάζειν παρὰ νηυσὶ κορωνίσιν, οὔ οἱ ἔπειτα
ἄρκιον ἐσσεῖται φυγέειν κύνας ἠδ' οἰωνούς.

'and as for anyone I see who prefers to loiter by the beaked ships far from battle, nothing can save him: he is for the dogs and birds'? The same organising principle is valid also for the Trojans, who in the epic differ only slightly from the Greeks in tactical training and competence, as in their weapons and domestic arrangements (cf. Helbig, op. cit., pp. 5, 13). The poet adds a powerful reason for it when he has Iris say in B 803ff.: πολλοὶ γὰρ κατὰ ἄστυ μέγα Πριάμου ἐπίκουροι, ἄλλη δ' ἄλλων γλῶσσα πολυσπερέων ἀνθρώπων 'in his great town, Priam has many allies. But these scattered foreigners all speak different languages'; 'therefore' (she goes on) 'everyone should be in command of those he rules, and lead his compatriots out to battle after he has drawn them up in order'.

After Agamemnon has announced the decision to fight, he orders the assembly to disperse so that everyone may prepare a meal in his tent, get his weapons ready, feed the horses and so prepare to fight for the whole day until nightfall, B 381ff. So the men arm themselves in their tents, sacrifice and pray, each to one of the gods, for protection of their lives, 400-1, while the commander in chief summons the γέροντας ἀριστῆας Παναχαιῶν, 404 'the senior councillors of the Greeks', to implore Zeus in solemn sacrifice for support in the coming battle. After the sacrifice, on Agamemnon's command, heralds announce through the whole camp with resonant voices that the Achaeans should go to the mustering-place, 442ff., while the leaders go round the camp, urging slackers to hurry up, separating already the different contingents and preparing for the marshalling at the mustering-place, 446. This place was situated outside the camp – 465 ἐς πεδίον προχέοντο Σκαμάνδριον 'they poured onto the plain of the Scamander' – and **[I.8]** only there did the main task of the leaders, the κοσμήτορες λαῶν 'marshals of the people' begin. For the men were not led out there already formed into smaller or larger groups by junior officers so that they could quickly take their proper places within the larger muster, but in wild confusion (just as swans and cranes fly to and fro with loud screeching) they made their way in immense throngs to the Scamandrian meadow. The leaders now had to seek out their own men, just as shepherds διακρίνωσιν 'sort out' their flocks, ἐπεί κε νομῷ μιγέωσιν, 475, 'when they have become mixed up at pasture' and then to lead them to their place in the plain under the supreme command of Agamemnon, 477; just as it is said of Ajax in 558 στῆσε δ᾽ ἄγων ἵν᾽ Ἀθηναίων ἵσταντο φάλαγγες 'he brought them to the place where the Athenian forces stood.' The poet shows us in the ἐπιπώλησις 'tour of inspection' of Agamemnon how he imagines the line-up of the individual tribes, and in this way offers us in truly poetic fashion a vivid picture without tiring us with a bare list.

The same method of preparation for battle is also assumed on the following battle-days, although the picture is not drawn in such detail again, but only sketched in with a few strokes. So, immediately after, it is said much more briefly of Hector and his Trojans in B 808: αἶψα δ᾽ ἔλυσ᾽ ἀγορήν. ἐπὶ τεύχεα δ᾽ ἐσσεύοντο 'He immediately dismissed the assembly. They rushed to arms', then the gates are opened and out pour the men in noisy confusion, 810, to the broad-based κολώνη Βατίεια, ἔνθα τότε Τρῶές τε διέκριθεν ἠδ᾽ ἐπίκουροι 815 'Bramble Hill ... it was here that the Trojans and their allies were marshalled for battle'. This certainly does not just mean 'the Trojans were separated from the allies', but the sixteen contingents listed in lines 816-77 are separated and drawn up by their leaders, Γ 1 κόσμηθεν ἅμ᾽ ἡγεμόνεσσιν ἕκαστοι 'they were drawn up, each contingent under its leader'. The course of events on the second day of battle is similarly, though even more briefly, described at Θ 53ff.:

οἱ δ᾽ ἄρα δεῖπνον ἕλοντο κάρη κομόωντες Ἀχαιοὶ
ῥίμφα κατὰ κλισίας, ἀπὸ δ᾽ αὐτοῦ θωρήσσοντο.
Τρῶες δ᾽ αὖθ᾽ ἑτέρωθεν ἀνὰ πτόλιν ὡπλίζοντο

'Meanwhile the long-haired Greeks snatched a meal in their huts and then armed; while on the other side, in the town, the Trojans also prepared themselves for battle' and all the gates were opened and out poured the men in noisy confusion, 59. The sequence of events is just the same on the third day of battle, Λ 15: Ἀτρείδης δ᾽ ἐβόησεν ἰδὲ ζώννυσθαι ἄνωγεν Ἀργείους 'Agamemnon shouted orders to his troops to prepare for battle'; there follows the drawing up of the Greeks at the ditch 47-52; and at 56 it is said: Τρῶες δ᾽ αὖθ᾽ ἑτέρωθεν ἐπὶ θρωσμῷ πεδίοιο sc. ἐκόσμηθεν 'On their side too the Trojans lined up on the high ground of the plain'. At Π 155 Homer describes how Achilles draws up the Myrmidons for battle on behalf of Patroclus, Μυρμιδόνας δ᾽ ἄρ᾽ ἐποιχόμενος θώρηξεν Ἀχιλλεὺς πάντας ἀνὰ κλισίας σὺν τεύχεσιν 'Achilles went the rounds of the huts and got all his Myrmidons under arms'; their leaders hurry about while this is happening, helpfully lending Achilles a hand, 164ff.

αὐτὰρ ἐπειδὴ πάντας ἅμ' ἡγεμόνεσσιν Ἀχιλλεὺς
στῆσεν ἐΰ κρίνας, κρατερὸν δ' ἐπὶ μῦθον ἔτελλεν.

'When Achilles had drawn them all up, men with their commanders
in their proper ranks, he addressed them bluntly' (198-9). In T 230ff.,
before Achilles moves into battle with the Greek army after Patroclus'
death, Odysseus says in the assembly: all those who are going into
battle should first μεμνῆσθαι πόσιος καὶ ἐδητύος, ὄφρ' ἔτι μᾶλλον ...
μαχώμεθα ... ἑσσάμενοι χροῒ χαλκὸν ἀτειρέα 'turn their thoughts to food
and drink, so that we can carry on the struggle without let-up ... with
our bronze armour – that never tires – on our backs'; then, after
Agamemnon has dismissed the assembly, everyone goes to his tent,
276, and Ἀχαιοὶ ... θωρήσσοντο κατὰ στρατόν 352 'the Greeks were
arming themselves throughout the camp'; then 356 τοὶ δ' ἀπάνευθε
νεῶν ἐχέοντο θοάων 'the troops poured out from among the swift ships',
and further Υ 1-3 ὣς οἱ μὲν ... θωρήσσοντο ... Ἀχαιοί, Τρῶες δ' αὖθ'
ἑτέρωθεν ἐπὶ θρωσμῷ πεδίοιο 'So the Greeks armed for battle ..., and on
the other side the Trojans too were arming on the high ground of the
plain'.

So the sequence of preparations for battle is this: after the order
given by the commander in chief, the men arm themselves in their
tents and essentially without any order flock to the mustering-place;
there the κρίνειν and κοσμεῖν 'sorting out and drawing up' take place;
and then the men advance **[I.9]** into battle. Therefore, when it is said
at the end of Iris' speech in B 805-6: τοῖσιν ἕκαστος ἀνὴρ σημαινέτω,
οἷσί περ ἄρχει, τῶν δ' ἐξηγείσθω κοσμησάμενος πολιήτας 'Let their own
commanders in each case issue orders to them, draw up their people
and lead them out to battle', we cannot with Ameis-Hentze interpret
τῶν δ' ἐξηγείσθω 'lead them out' which was preceded by κοσμεῖσθαι
'draw up' as 'lead out of the city onto the battle field' because the
ordering and drawing up take place only outside the walls; but the
verb ἐξηγείσθω, found only here, 'let them lead out', is synonymous
with σημαινέτω 'let them issue orders' in the previous line and with
the expressions ἡγεμονεύειν 'be in charge of' and ἄρχειν 'lead' which
follow later, 816, 819 (and often). With Faesi-Franke, it should be
interpreted generally as 'lead out to battle'. πολιήτας can then in this
context only mean 'their people' and not, as La Roche wants, 'the citizens, inhabitants of Troy'. Since the instruction given by Iris that
everyone should lead his own countrymen is so general, it seems to me
that it is self-evidently included that the Trojans are commanded by
Trojan leaders (as we find in all the battle scenes), and the express
mention of this consequence, which La Roche finds missing, does not
seem absolutely necessary.

When the men set out to be marshalled on the third day of battle,

27

we find something which had been wholly disregarded on the second day, the camp surrounded by a rampart and a deep ditch. Perhaps we momentarily assume that the marshalling, so that it could be carried out under secure protection, took place in the space between the rampart and the ditch, which we must imagine to be quite wide. But this is not the case; the army first crosses the ditch in no order, and is then drawn up on the other side. As one can very well understand, the ditch formed an absolute obstacle to the advance of an army in battle order, and was therefore crossed by the individual soldiers at places which seemed convenient to them. When the leaders too drove out to the mustering-place, they found cause to dismount on their side of the ditch and cross on foot, with the chariots following slowly behind, Λ 47ff. This, likewise, obviously excludes the possibility that the whole army could cross if it had already been drawn up. There is not the slightest hint anywhere in the epic that people feared an attack by the opposing forces while the army was being drawn up, even though such a time would have been an excellent opportunity for this; if an engagement of that sort had been a feature of battle at that time, I do not think that a poet would have missed the chance of describing it. I would see the reason for this in the fact that, with the extremely limited mobility of massed troops – and a successful attack could be carried out only *en masse* – both parties needed considerable time to draw up their armies. Night regularly breaks off the battle, but to marshal the troops you really must have daylight. So the safest thing was that, when one had decided on battle, one went to the marshalling at first light as soon as the other preparations had been made, and both sides began battle early. And so it actually says on the second and third battle-day Θ 66-7, Λ 84-5:

ὄφρα μὲν ἠὼς ἦν καὶ ἀέξετο ἱερὸν ἦμαρ,
τόφρα μάλ᾿ ἀμφοτέρων βέλε᾿ ἥπτετο.

'Right through the morning, while the blessed light of day grew stronger, volley and counter-volley found their mark'. Again, on the fourth day of battle, Thetis brings her son his weapons into the camp T 1ff. when dawn breaks; whereas on the first day a slight postponement had naturally occurred.

Drawing up the men is an art which belongs to the leader, the κοσμήτορι λαῶν 'marshal of the people', and constitutes an appreciable part of his leadership skills: for the army can be used only after it has been drawn up (cf. Köchly and Rüstow, *Kriegswesen*, p. 6). It is for this **[I.10]** that Menestheus is richly praised, B 553-4, for τῷ δ᾿ οὔ πώ τις ὁμοῖος ἐπιχθόνιος γένετ᾿ ἀνὴρ κοσμῆσαι ἵππους τε καὶ ἀνέρας ἀσπιδιώτας 'he had no rival on earth in the art of drawing up infantry and chariots'. Most important was the formation of the front line in the contingent.[4] For it was here, as it was with the Roman legions in battle, that the first decisive step could be taken towards a favourable outcome or its opposite, if they succeeded in breaking through the enemy's front line – all the more so in Homer, since there were no troops to be called up from reserve. Therefore all those had to stand in the first line who, through physical strength and skill, through confidence and courage, were most capable of standing up to the enemy's attempt to break through, or of hurling themselves valiantly at the enemy line. In the 'standing fight', the warriors would leap out from the first row, as πρόμαχοι 'front line fighters'[5] to kill an individual opponent or hurl their spear into the enemy ranks; in the front line, as well as the best of their men, stood all the leaders and heroes whose names the poet has made immortal, leading all the others as shining examples of heroic courage in war, and giving the ordinary troops both command and example to act bravely and resolutely. But in the front line the best *armed* men also had to stand (for it must be regarded as proven that there were differently armed men even within individual contingents) and the author of the somewhat peculiar exchange of weapons, Ξ 376ff., which Poseidon carries out before he leads the Greeks into battle, quite probably had this point in mind, that, for the drawing up of the battle line, consideration of the weapons was of especially great importance and might not infrequently be the decisive factor, even in comparison with personal prowess. It says there: ὃς δέ κ' ἀνὴρ μενέχαρμος 'every warrior who is steadfast in battle', i.e. who can sustain an attack, should take the larger shield, which was more suitable for this purpose, and should give his small shield to the inferior man. The men obey this order, 378, then the leaders draw up the troops for attack, 379, ἐκόσμεον 'they drew them up', thereby effecting the exchange of arms, and after that Poseidon moves to the attack. Incidentally, I am far from thinking that this attempt at explanation removes all the reservations one has about this passage; I have merely wanted to hazard a guess about its origin, in the context of our present question.

The battle lines standing behind the first one are expressly referred to several times: Δ 253-4 Ἰδομενεὺς μὲν ἐνὶ προμάχοις ... Μηριόνης δ' ἄρα οἱ πυμάτας ὤτρυνε φάλαγγας 'In the forefront was Idomeneus ... while Meriones urged on the troops at the rear', Λ 64-5 Ἕκτωρ ὅτε μέν τε μετὰ πρώτοισι φάνεσκεν, ἄλλοτε δ' ἐν πυμάτοισι κελεύων 'Hector was seen, now in the front ranks, now in the rear, spurring them on'; at N 131-3 and Π 215-17 it is described how in the formation which has been closed up to fend off the enemy attack, the men stand closely behind each other ὣς πυκνοὶ ἐφέστασαν ἀλλήλοισιν 'so close were the ranks'; in Δ 281-2 it is said of the forces of the two Ajaxes, which have already been drawn up and are in the process of advancing, πυκιναὶ ... φάλαγγες σάκεσίν τε καὶ ἔγχεσι πεφρικυῖαι 'the close-packed ranks ... bristling with shields and spears', something which can be said only about a considerable number of lines marching behind each other with their spears raised. Of several other passages which are relevant here, I wish briefly to quote and discuss one more, Δ 297ff. which presents us with Nestor, the most experienced marshal of men, in action:

ἱππῆας μὲν πρῶτα σὺν ἵπποισιν καὶ ὄχεσφι,
πεζοὺς δ᾽ ἐξόπιθε στῆσεν πολέας τε καὶ ἐσθλούς,
ἕρκος ἔμεν πολέμοιο, κακοὺς δ᾽ ἐς μέσσον ἔλασσεν,
ὄφρα καὶ οὐκ ἐθέλων τις ἀναγκαίῃ πολεμίζοι.

'Nestor stationed his charioteers with their horses and chariots in the front and behind them his many brave foot-soldiers, for defence in battle. He placed his inferior troops in the middle so that even the unwilling would be forced to fight'. It had to matter to Nestor, and of course to every other leader in the same position, to bring above all as many of his foot-soldiers as possible for deployment in battle, even those who did not show any great courage. Therefore he had to place in the front **[I.11]** line the competent and tried and tested men, as also in the rear line, which had to move up to make a tightly closed column for attack or defence and to prevent the weaker brethren, who were standing in the middle, from breaking out; in this way, the faint-hearted in the middle were forced to stand firm by those in front and behind. Such compulsion must also have seemed to be necessary when Agamemnon proposed that they should pull some of the ships down into the sea during the battle and the rest at night with the aim of flight, and Odysseus, Ξ 99, could object that the Achaeans would no longer stand firm in battle the moment they noticed that the ships were being pulled down into the sea behind them.

The interpretation of the passage at Δ 297 by Köpke, op. cit., p. 220 and in agreement with him Friedreich p. 386 does at first sight seem to be the correct one, i.e. that he 'placed the chariots at the front, the best of the foot-soldiers at the back and the cowards in the middle between them and the charioteers'. But it seems utterly untenable to me. For firstly, in our passage it is not the case that the ἱππῆες, the πεζοί and the κακοί 'charioteers, foot-soldiers and inferior troops' are contrasted groups, but only the former two; the κακοί 'inferior troops' belong to the πεζοί 'foot-soldiers', and therefore logically one cannot take ἐς μέσσον 'into the middle' with ἱππήων καὶ πεζῶν 'charioteers and foot-soldiers' but only with πεζῶν 'foot-soldiers'. And secondly, the κακοί 'inferior troops' would in this way constitute the first line of the πεζοί 'foot-soldiers' which is of course not intended, since it seems to me quite inconceivable in real life that the charioteers constitute the first line of the formation and therefore must proceed at the same speed as the infantry. For in that way, the main advantage which they have compared with infantry, their speed, would be completely lost, and as the first part of an infantry formation they would lose any mobility and thus the greatest part of their usefulness in battle. Moreover, if that were the case, how would an ἀναχωρεῖν 'dropping behind' of individual chariots, which Nestor 305 expressly forbids, be conceivable at all?

The epic gives no hint whatsoever about the depth of the formation, which even in the Dorian phalanx was by no means constant and seems to have varied between four and six men, later up to eight. We shall not go wrong if we assume that in this respect no fixed practice prevailed. If our explanation given above of Δ 299 ἐς μέσσον 'into the middle' is correct, we have to assume at least three lines behind each other, a number which is probably too low when one considers that a deeper formation would make it considerably easier to maintain the order and cohesiveness of the formation when advancing.

Presumably the closeness of the battle order was usually not very great, since the distance of the individual warriors from each other had to be far enough for a man to be able to brandish and throw his spear from his position in the line. For not only do individual heroes leap forward and throw, but a kind of salvo too is launched by many at the same time, as proof of which I refer to the splendid description of an attack O 306ff. The Achaeans had adopted an orderly formation to cover their retreat, ὑσμίνην ἤρτυνον ... Ἕκτορι καὶ Τρώεσσιν ἐναντίον 'they formed a strong battle-line against Hector and the Trojans', the Trojans advanced in a dense throng, προὔτυψαν ἀολλέες 'they burst forward in mass formation', and the former awaited the attack in large numbers as well, ὑπέμειναν ἀολλέες 'they awaited them in mass formation'. Then a loud battle cry is raised on both sides, 'and arrows fly from the bowstrings, and numerous spears are hurled by mighty hands, some of which hit their mark and some, having fallen short of their target, get stuck in the ground between the two battle lines', 317. For the same reason the second and third lines could not move up too closely either; on the other hand it would be completely wrong to imagine the distance between them to be as great as Friedreich does, who on p. 386 says: 'the separate lines do not seem to have stood very close to each other; but rather, between them there seems to have existed a space which without doubt was described by the word γέφυρα 'bridge'; this interval was not small since horses and chariots moved **[I.12]** within it'. Now one certainly cannot understand the γέφυραι 'bridges' (which have not yet been adequately explained) as longitudinal sections, but at most as cross-sections of the battle line.

But apart from that, a space of that kind, especially if chariots drive through it, would completely destroy order and coherence. If, during the battle, an advance was suddenly made by the enemy, who in the σταδίη μάχη 'standing fight' were standing at a distance of thirty to forty paces away at most, it would have been utterly impossible for the lines then to close quickly together from right and left and from the rear to the front to the place which was threatened so that shield overlapped with shield and the helmet crests touched each other (see below).[6]

The lines which have been drawn up in order are called στίχες 'ranks', between which the leaders move during the drawing-up or the advance Δ 231, 250, Ο 279. These move forward Ρ 107, are attacked Λ 264, 540, broken through Ν 680, put to flight Ρ 505. But one should hardly conclude from the fact that Achilles drew up his Myrmidons in five στίχες 'ranks' Π 171ff. πέντε δ' ἄρ' ἡγεμόνας ποιήσατο ... τῆς μὲν ἰῆς στιχὸς ἦρχε Μενέσθιος ... τῆς δ' ἑτέρης Εὔδωρος κ. τ. λ. 'He had appointed five commanders ... Menesthius led the first line ... Eudorus the second line etc.' that he drew up his formation five men deep. On the contrary, we can very well see from the verses which follow soon after how the poet imagined a typical marshalling of the troops. For when the Myrmidons, who have been drawn up by Achilles, are spurred on by his words and want once more to show themselves at their best to their beloved leader before they set out for battle, it says in Π 211ff.: the lines closed up more tightly,

μᾶλλον δὲ στίχες ἄρθεν, ἐπεὶ βασιλῆος ἄκουσαν.
ὡς δ' ὅτε τοῖχον ἀνὴρ ἀράρῃ πυκινοῖσι λίθοισι
δώματος ὑψηλοῖο, βίας ἀνέμων ἀλεείνων,
ὣς ἄραρον κόρυθές τε καὶ ἀσπίδες ὀμφαλόεσσαι κ. τ. λ.

'The ranks closed when they heard their lord. As a mason fits together blocks of stone when he builds the wall of a high house to make sure of keeping out the wind, so tightly packed were their helmets and their bossed shields, etc.' So the unit must be drawn up in close formation. The intervals between the lines mentioned above as being necessary doubtless occurred automatically as soon as they started moving. Then the lines opened out in all directions; for the troops known to the epic poets had certainly not yet been drilled for a parade march in line abreast, and we know how difficult it is even for drilled soldiers to keep precisely in line whilst marching forwards. But the heroic formation was not only not trained, it was not even uniformly armed or equipped. Some carried larger shields, longer spears, better armour than others; indeed, evidently not all the warriors who stood in the formation carried shield and spear; but some were armed with bows. This is expressly mentioned of several leaders, Pandarus, Paris, Teucer; and also clearly follows from the passage quoted above, Ο 306ff., where arrows fly in a salvo at the same time as spears. Hector is also shot at with arrows from the lines of the Greeks in Γ 80 when he steps out in front of the Trojan army. Later on I shall have to make further brief mention of the Locrians of Ajax who carry only the bow.

Since the drawing up was important for the battle-readiness of the men, it was certainly a friendly act performed by Achilles for Patroclus before his departure for battle, that he personally directed the arming and drawing up of the Myrmidons, which takes place in the manner mentioned above with the assistance of Patroclus and the subordinate commanders, 164ff.: Μυρμιδόνων ἡγήτορες ἠδὲ μέδοντες ἀμφ᾽ ἀγαθὸν θεράποντα ... Αἰακίδαο ῥώοντ᾽ κ. τ. λ., 'the captains and commanders of the Myrmidons surged forward around Achilles' brave lieutenant'. When this has been completed it is followed, as almost always, by a speech from the leader encouraging the men to be valiant (this has rightly been compared elsewhere with the *adhortatio* customary among the Romans before battle).

[I.13] However, the view which Köpke expresses about the marshalling, op. cit., p. 218, and Friedreich p. 386, who follows him verbatim, seems to me utterly impossible to prove: 'We find that not only is it stressed several times that similarly equipped forces are drawn up together, but we may also assume that similar troops were drawn up in positions where they would fight against men armed in the same way opposite them. See *Il.* XI 150 f. where it is said: "Now infantry were slaughtering infantry, driven back in flight, and charioteers were slaughtering charioteers etc." ' For, quite apart from the fact that in the epic there is no trace of the deployment of differently armed troops as such, even the passage cited, Λ 150ff., does not seem to me at all to support the conclusions drawn from it, i.e. that, incredibly, either both armies would have to agree to draw up their troops in accordance with the different types of their weapons, or that a definitely fixed rule about this must have existed (as it did, for instance, in the Roman army, where the light-armed troops and the cavalry go to the wings). The subject there is the Trojans' wild flight from victorious Agamemnon and his men; the former try to escape, if possible, the latter to do as much damage to the enemy as they can. It is a wholly natural consequence, from which nothing can be concluded about the formation of chariot squadrons, that during this the ἱππῆες 'chariot fighters', who had mounted their chariots, pursue those of the enemy who are fleeing on chariots, because they alone can catch them, and because the killing of a noble brought more profit than that of a common man (I understand by ἱππῆες 'chariot fighters' only the leaders and nobles; this will be dealt with in the next section). Thus in Π 382-3 Patroclus on his chariot pursues the fleeing Hector in particular, τὸν δ᾽ ἔκφερον ὠκέες ἵπποι, 'but Hector's swift horses carried him to safety', and in this way eventually gets in front of the fleeing Trojan foot-soldiers, whom he partly cuts off and drives back.

These scenes however are taking us into the middle of the battle itself; and before we pass on to that – or even just allow the drawn-up contingents to advance into battle – another particularly important question must be settled, viz. that of the use of chariots in Homeric battles.

Use of Chariots

In line with the general organisation of the army discussed above, as we find it everywhere in the epic, it should be accepted that there were no chariot squadrons as a separate force distinct from the tribal units; when chariot squadrons are mentioned, these can only be the chariots provided by a particular tribe, and these chariots would be attached to that same tribe when they were being drawn up and during the battle. That a tribe provided only ἵπποι 'chariot troops' could at best be true of the Thracians, who are mentioned at K 473 but are virtually insignificant in the narrative. We are given reliable information about the drawing up of such chariot squadrons in one particular case – the instructions that Nestor gives his chariot fighters in Δ 297ff. It was certainly deliberate that the venerable Pylian of all people should have these precepts put in his mouth, since chariot fighters could probably be found more plentifully represented in the contingent from Pylos, which was an area rich in horses. The oriental custom of using chariots in battle surely spread earliest to the Peloponnese, and, [I.14] as Helbig, op. cit., p. 89 indicates, this must have happened before the Dorian migration, since battle chariots are represented on Mycenaean grave monuments. So the poet rightly credits old ἱππότα 'charioteer' Nestor with the richest experience in the use of ἵπποι 'horses' both here and in other passages:

'So the chariot fighters are to advance in tight formation; no one is to drive out of it to fight an individual opponent; no one is to drop behind the line; when the chariots have thus reached the enemy squadrons in close order, let each man aim from his chariot at the enemy opposite, since this is the best way to achieve success; this was the fighting method with which the men of past times gained their victories.'

So Nestor's main emphasis is on the close order of the chariot squadrons, and he forbids individual combat. In doing so, he presupposes that his opponents likewise are chariot fighters and observe the same rules. This instruction must appear thoroughly sound and practical, and shows that the poet of this passage had formed for himself a clear notion of the use of chariot fighters. But, curiously enough, not only have these chariot fighters forgotten this sound piece of advice immediately afterwards when the battle begins – something to which Köpke pp. 221 and 147 rightly draws attention – but these 'squadrons' do not play any part in the battle at all. Not only in the battle scenes which immediately follow is their use as a first-wave strike-force to prepare for the attack of the infantry completely ignored, but in all the battle scenes and descriptions of fighting before Troy which the epic presents to us, chariot squadrons are used neither to begin an attack, nor for direct assault, nor for pursuit, nor for any military purpose at all. The only description of a real battle between chariot squadrons is put in old Nestor's mouth as a tale from his youth, Λ 711-61, a passage which is now, of course, for quite different reasons, generally regarded as a spurious interpolation. In other passages too, mounted squadrons are mentioned quite generally, or can be understood by the mention of ἵπποι 'horses', e.g. I 383-4, as proof of the splendid might of Egyptian Thebes in Achilles' speech, where twenty thousand chariot fighters issue forth from its hundred gates (a passage whose authenticity is likewise in doubt); H 240 οἶδα δ' ἐπαΐξαι μόθον ἵππων ὠκειάων 'I know how to charge in among the confusion of chariots'; Λ 529-30 ἔνθα μάλιστα ... ἱππῆες πεζοί τε ... ἀλλήλους ὀλέκουσι 'where especially ... the charioteers and infantry ... are killing each other'; Π 810 φῶτας ἐείκοσι βῆσεν ἀφ' ἵππων πρῶτ' ἐλθὼν σὺν ὄχεσφι 'in the first battle he had fought with his chariot, he brought down twenty men from their chariots'; P 175 οὗτοι ἐγὼν ἔρριγα μάχην οὐδὲ κτύπον ἵππων 'Believe me, fighting and the noise of chariots do not frighten me'; Υ 326 πολλὰς δὲ στίχας ἡρώων, πολλὰς δὲ καὶ ἵππων Αἰνείας ὑπεράλτο 'Aeneas vaulted over all the intervening lines of infantry and charioteers'. In the passages B 810, Λ 51-2 which will be further discussed below, Λ 151, if it is genuine, and M 62, Σ 237, I understand by ἵπποι 'horses' and ἱππῆες 'charioteers' only the chariot drivers in the service of the leaders and nobles who are proceeding independently; likewise Ψ 132, where a greater number of ἱππῆες 'charioteers' evidently only appear to enhance the pomp of Patroclus' funeral, but have nothing to do with the fighting. But the view which is expressed in *Odyssey* σ 261: Τρῶας ... ἔμμεναι ... ἵππων τ' ὠκυπόδων ἐπιβήτορας, οἵ κε τάχιστα ἔκριναν μέγα νεῖκος ὁμοιίου πολέμοιο 'that the Trojans are riders of swift-footed horses, which can tip the scales in an evenly matched battle more quickly than anything,' does not find confirmation in the descriptions in the *Iliad*. The use of chariots, as it appears here, is organically linked with the battle scenes and comes to us in vivid and graphic description right down to the details; it is different, and much more limited. The main emphasis in battle is without doubt on the foot-soldiers, especially those armed with breastplate, shield, sword and spear; however, the use of chariot fighters in an integrated squadron still appears known to the poet, perhaps from memory through songs or tales, but no longer from personal observation. The development of **[I.15]** warfare at the time of the composition of the epic had already taken a step further into that of the time which followed, in which hoplites alone fought out the battle, and chariot fighting was completely abandoned.

On the other hand, beside these merely generalised references to chariot squadrons, there regularly appear individual leaders and nobles in chariots, playing a prominent role in all the battle descriptions, though not in large numbers, as the list in Hopf, op. cit., Progr. 1858 p. 2 and p. 35 shows. But these can absolutely not be given the name chariot fighters. Since they are armed with the heavier shield (cf. Helbig pp. 222, 250), breastplate and greaves, and since the demands on their mobility during the drawing up of the army, as in battle, are quite different from those on their men, they use the chariot mainly in order to do justice to their various tasks as leaders, especially before and after the actual battle. They differ from chariot squadrons, if I may use the comparison, roughly in the same way as the mounted officers of the infantry differ from the cavalry; but cavalry is not used in the battles before Ilium.

The question of the use of chariots in war makes a separate discussion necessary, since earlier analyses known to me deviate in my opinion considerably from the state of affairs represented in the epic. In Köchly and Rüstow, op. cit., p. 6, we read on this matter: 'The positioning of the chariot fighters – treated as cavalry – in relation to the foot-soldiers results from the overall interconnections of the two groups. The leaders belong in front of their men, especially if they wish to act as champions. As a result, the chariots naturally position themselves in the front line in normal circumstances whether the poet emphasises this or not, and only exceptionally does it happen that they are placed on the wings, in which case infantry advances against infantry, chariots against chariots.' But the statement, which is probably correct in individual points, is not acceptable as a generalisation like this. Likewise, what Buchholz, op. cit., p. 311 says about chariot fighters is almost totally a figment of his imagination. Again, Köpke's view (p. 146ff.) about the three possible ways of drawing up the chariot squadrons (and Friedreich's, who again agrees with him verbatim, p. 368) is only an interpretation derived from Δ 303 and Λ 49ff. as well as 150ff. The first, Nestor's instruction, has already been discussed above. We shall now have to dwell on the second for a moment. It proves nothing about the drawing up of chariot squadrons in a second line behind the infantry, as was deduced by Köpke and firmly accepted by Helbig p. 88, however attractive the supporting argument appears: 'The Greeks, who had been driven back the day before and were now prepared for an attack at any time, advanced from their defensive fortifications and therefore could not bring their chariots into play immediately; the chariots, however, were able to take up a position, undisturbed and unnoticed, behind the infantry, and so to give them the most effective support.' But in Λ 47ff., the description of the march out on the third battle-day, we are not dealing with mounted squadrons at all, but (and in this I agree with most of the commentators, from whom I differ only on one unimportant point) with the leaders and nobles who travel to the mustering-place on their chariots – the same leaders who, after the marshalling of the army, appear in the battle on foot together with their men. For the verses Λ 47-9 when put together with the almost identical ones in M 76-7 (Polydamas' advice) can only mean that the chariot drivers are to stop on the near side of the ditch, as their commanders intend to cross it on foot. They then draw up their men on the other side of the ditch with **[I.16]** a great deal of noise, which was emphasised sufficiently at its first mention B 459ff.; for this is what the expression ῥώοντο 50 'they bustled' means here, as it does in the similar situation in Π 166 when the Myrmidons are drawn up. Then in verse 51 it continues: they, the leaders, however, were drawn up at the ditch, i.e. with their men – now on the far side, of course – far sooner than the chariot drivers who had to take their places behind the line close to their commanders; I then translate 52 ἱππῆες δ' ὀλίγον μετεκίαθον 'the chariot drivers arrived a little later', i.e. at the mustering-place, because the crossing of the ditch had delayed them (unlike most commentators of the passage who translate: 'they followed them at a short distance'). For an advance of the two armies is not in question here at all; that begins only after the Trojans also have finished their drawing up, 56ff., around line 67; besides, ὀλίγον 'a little' is not used elsewhere by Homer in a local sense, but usually serves to denote degree, especially with a comparative, and ὀλίγον μετεκίαθον means: 'they came a little later' (cf. also La Roche *Stud.* para. 29, who however takes ὀλίγον in this single passage in a local sense). This is, of course, an extremely simple interpretation – not fundamentally different from Franke's and Hentze's views – but there is nothing more to the verses, and the drawing up of chariot squadrons in a second line of battle cannot be deduced from them.

How then are chariots used in the poem itself? Helbig essentially hits the nail on the head when he briefly says, p. 89, 'the chariot really serves as a base for either advance or retreat', and for a relatively small number of leaders and nobles at that. Not all the leaders and not only leaders are provided with chariots, although it seems to have been a kind of requirement for their position. Pandarus, for example, says to Aeneas, Ŀ 199, that his father earnestly urged him ἵπποισιν ... καὶ ἅρμασιν ἐμβεβαῶτα ἀρχεύειν Τρώεσσι κατὰ κρατερὰς ὑσμίνας 'to lead his men into the thick of the action on a horse-drawn chariot'. But we know that Pandarus had left his horses at home because he feared a fodder shortage; how then, if a royal leader had to be worried about such matters, were whole cavalry squadrons supposed to find their food?

The leader uses his chariot firstly to ride to the mustering-place of his people, where he leaves it to marshal them, inspect them or spur them on with a speech. During the advance to battle (unless it starts immediately after the drawing up), he is usually located on his chariot behind the line, but in any case he leaves it immediately the battle begins; indeed, his alighting from the chariot is really to be regarded as a sign that the hero now intends to participate in the battle. For this reason alone, the chariots cannot move along in front of the ranks of fighters, as Rüstow thought, since they would only constitute an obstacle. Only in very few individual instances, during flight and pursuit, do warriors actually fight from their chariots. The pretty picture which the poet presents to us in a few verses, O 385-9, where he has the Greeks fighting from their ships and the Trojans from their chariots, is taken from a pursuit scene, but is moreover disregarded immediately afterwards in the subsequent descriptions (cf. on this also Hentze's *Appendix* to O, Introduction p. 104).

The warriors mount their chariots again when the battle line has been broken and a moment of crisis reached; on the part of the vanquished, in order to escape the danger, which at this moment above all is particularly great, through rapid flight, on that of the victors, to damage the enemy in immediate pursuit and, if possible, to kill an outstanding leader or a noble, resplendent in his luxurious armour. That is why Aeneas Ŀ 223 extols the outstanding ability of his horses when it is necessary κραιπνὰ μάλ᾽ ἔνθα καὶ ἔνθα διωκέμεν ἠδὲ φέβεσθαι 'quickly to cover the ground in pursuit or retreat', and Ajax N 819 mockingly shouts at Hector that he will soon **[I.17]** beseech Father Zeus for his horses to be swifter than hawks when they carry him to the city in hasty flight. If the opponent's success is not a decisive one which demands swift flight, and the warriors fight as they retreat, chariots are not mounted – only when the retreat degenerates into flight. If the battle turns again from a rout to making a stand, then the leader, who will often have got far in front of his men because of the speed of his horses, leaves his chariot again to take part in the new battle on foot. But not all heroes provided with chariots use them only for swift flight. It is a proof of exceptional courage if a hero, after he has mounted his chariot, dares to drive head-on against a victorious, advancing, opponent to delay his progress, an action which is quite common among the typical incidents in the descriptions of flight and pursuit.

To show that the use of ἵπποι 'horses' outlined above is the one which regularly forms the basis of the descriptions in the epic, let us now look at a number of passages from the poem itself (though we shall not be able to avoid repeatedly touching on issues of advance, attack, flight and pursuit which are really meant to be discussed later).

The situation at the beginning of Book 3 shows the positions of leader and chariot during the advance into battle. When drawing up has been completed, both armies advance against each other, prepared for battle. When they have come close to each other, Γ 15, Menelaus catches sight of Paris, 21, who was ostentatiously striding ahead of the Trojans and challenging the Greek heroes to a duel. Delighted that the opportunity to take revenge on the offender has come at last, he leaps from his chariot ready to fight, 29: αὐτίκα δ᾿ ἐξ ὀχέων σὺν τεύχεσιν ἆλτο χαμᾶζε 'Fully armed, he immediately leapt from his chariot to the ground'. But when Paris noticed him ἐν προμάχοισι φανέντα, κατεπλήγη φίλον ἦτορ, 31 *'emerging through the front ranks*, his heart failed him completely' and he retreated into the company of his comrades. So Menelaus was not yet ἐν προμάχοισι 'in the front ranks', but had caught sight of Paris from his chariot; he jumps down only because he wants to begin the fight with him and suddenly appears in the front line, to Paris' dismay.

When Paris has later agreed to the duel, Hector steps out in the middle in front of the Trojans, 77, and pushes their lines back with his spear. So in this instance, as under very similar circumstances before the duel between Hector and Ajax, H 55ff., the idea that the chariots of the leaders could in any way be in front of the army is utterly impossible. After Menelaus' declaration, 97-110, which he makes standing in front of the army, the Achaean and Trojan leaders leave their chariots, 113, and they all sit down 'like a great assembly of umpires' (Faesi) to watch the duel, for which, of course, the natural assumption is that the chariots are likewise standing behind the lines. It is also said of Priam and Antenor who came driving out of the city, 265-6 ἐξ ἵππων ἀποβάντες ... ἐς μέσσον Τρώων καὶ Ἀχαιῶν ἐστιχόωντο *'they stepped down from the chariot ...* and walked to a spot between the Greeks and Trojans', which surely means that they left their chariot where the other chariots were standing, and then went into the space between the two armies; this is a passage which should of course have importance attached to it only in the context of the whole situation.

As a result of Pandarus' fateful shot, the situation had changed completely. Both armies get ready for battle, and Agamemnon fulfils his responsibility as leader in full measure by spurring the men every-where to fight, Δ 223-5; ἵππους μὲν γὰρ ἔασε καὶ ἅρματα 'For he left aside his horses and chariot' (226), and the chariot driver kept them to one side, having been instructed to be ready at any time to take up the commander in chief if he was tired by his exertions, 230; 231 αὐτὰρ ὁ πεζὸς ἐὼν ἐπεπωλεῖτο στίχας ἀνδρῶν 'then he set out on foot to make his tour of inspection of the troops'.

During this ἐπιπώλησις 'tour of inspection', Agamemnon comes among others to the contingent of Diomedes whom he finds, 365, ἑσταότ' ἔν θ' ἵπποισι καὶ ἅρμασι κολλητοσι 'standing among the horses and finely-built chariots'; and next to him stands his **[I.18]** trusted chariot driver Sthenelus. So both are presumably ready to drive off at any moment in order to hurl themselves at an opponent? Not at all, for the poet continues:

καὶ τὸν μὲν νείκεσσεν ἰδὼν κρείων Ἀγαμέμνων ...
τί πτώσσεις, τί δ' ὀπιπεύεις πολέμοιο γεφύρας;
οὐ μὲν Τυδέϊ γ' ὧδε φίλον πτωσκαζέμεν ἦεν,
ἀλλὰ πολὺ πρὸ φίλων ἑτάρων δηΐοισι μάχεσθαι, κ. τ. λ.

'Seeing him, Agamemnon lord of men rebuked him ... "Why are you hanging back like this, just eyeing the lines of battle? It was not your father Tydeus' habit to hang back, but to come to grips with the enemy way out in front of his men"', etc. But why the serious reproaches for a hero who is ready to fight? The following verses give us the explanation. For when Sthenelus wants to reject Agamemnon's reproach as unjustified by referring to their earlier deeds at Thebes, Diomedes harshly addresses him, 411-12: Agamemnon is quite right to urge the Achaeans to battle 414, he says; this befits him as the commander in chief; ἀλλ' ἄγε δὴ καὶ νῶϊ μεδώμεθα θούριδος ἀλκῆς 'Come: time for *the two of us to call up that fighting spirit of ours!*' and with this he jumps down from his chariot, 419, to turn these words into deeds; and in 422ff. there follows the description of the clash between the two sides during which chariot fighters are not mentioned any-where. So Agamemnon's rebuke could appear justified because Diomedes was still on his chariot, i.e. not giving the impression that he wanted to hurl himself immediately into the battle which had already flared up elsewhere, but as if he was already preparing for flight from it – which, of course, was the last thing he had in mind.

In the battle itself Diomedes appears fighting on foot, Ε 13, and after his wounding he goes back to his chariot, 107, to have the arrow pulled out of his wound by Sthenelus; in 249 the latter advises him to mount his chariot and flee when Aeneas approaches. The fact that right at the beginning of the battle the brothers Phegeus and Idaeus drive on their chariot against Diomedes ahead of the other Trojans, Ε 12, is a unique event, which is shown to be more an act of stupidity than of bravery by Idaeus jumping down from the chariot after the death of his brother and running away, not making any attempt to protect his body, 21. After a short battle the Achaeans beat back the enemy, 37, and Agamemnon kills Odius who has already mounted his chariot and turned to flee, 39; and Idomeneus kills Phaestus, 46, who is just about to mount his chariot, because the Trojans are on the point of flight – a motif which is used frequently by the poet.

Hector, too, has mounted his chariot in the general rout, and it is only because Sarpedon's reproaches sting him that he jumps down and encourages the Trojans to renew the battle. They turn back, 497, and attack the Achaeans who wait for them courageously, 498; but when the Trojans make this turn, the Achaean chariot drivers immediately wheel round their horses, 505 (which so far had been triumphantly pursuing the Trojans, ahead of the infantry) and drive back behind the front through the lines of the Greeks who are getting themselves into formation, in order to clear the front for the battle which begins afresh soon after. Later, in the chapter on flight and pursuit, I shall try to justify more closely this interpretation of the passage, which differs from that of the commentators known to me.[7]

During the Trojan attack which now occurs under Hector's leadership, and with the assistance of Ares and Enyo, Ε 591ff., the Greeks slowly retreat at Diomedes' direction, 605, πρὸς Τρῶας τετραμμένοι αἰὲν ὀπίσσω εἴκετε 'Retreat then, but facing the enemy', cf. 699-702; only Menesthes and Anchialus, against orders, had mounted their chariot, evidently to flee, but they are both killed by Hector who comes up to them before they can get away, 608-9, cf. above Ε 12. All the other heroes mentioned as fighters appear on foot, Ajax 611, 615, 620 etc., Sarpedon 664, Tlepolemus 668, Hector 681. And it is also very significant that Hera and Athene, after their decision μεδώμεθα θούριδος ἀλκῆς 'let us call up that fighting spirit of ours!', **[I.19]** 718, should use the chariot only until they are near the field of battle, 775, and then mingle with the throng of battle on foot; Ares too fights on foot 849ff.

The fact that Diomedes, who was behind the line by his chariot cooling his wound 794ff., dared to mount and drive against the victorious Trojans when the Achaeans were retreating is a particularly brave action, which is here carried out at the express instruction of Athene (829) and with her support, and belongs to the recurring images in the description of a rout which were mentioned above. Only just before, Aeneas and Pandarus had shown the same heroic spirit.

But after the Trojans' resistance has been broken by the incursion of Ajax who in Ζ 6 Τρώων ῥῆξε φάλαγγα 'broke the Trojan line', they mount their chariots and wildly flee to the city, 41, or are killed on their chariots, 17ff. Hector too is on his chariot and jumps down only as a sign that the rout should end and the battle begin afresh under the protection of the wall, 103. The Trojans then turn and attack the Achaeans again, who this time do not stand up to them as before but at first retreat, 107. The scene between Glaucus and Diomedes which then follows, 119ff., is pretty well independent of the whole situation and treated as largely incidental. As verse 232 shows, they are both imagined on their chariots; one could say that this was because they were both just now in a situation of flight or pursuit, but all the same this passage cannot be regarded as proving my interpretation.

Encouraged by the return of Hector and Paris, H 1ff., the Trojans press forward afresh and Glaucus hits Iphinous (one of the three heroes mentioned by name whose killing is intended to illustrate the general success of the Trojans) as he is just jumping on to his chariot to take flight, 15 ἵππων ἐπιάλμενον ὠκειάων 'leaping up behind his fast mares'.

In Θ 77 Zeus had sown panic among the Greeks so that everyone flees; only Nestor stayed behind because his horse was wounded, 81; everybody else, as far as they were able, used their chariots to flee. Nestor's trace-horse had been hit in the head by Paris with a shot from in front, 82, and the two other horses must still be facing the Trojans, since Diomedes places himself, 100, protectively πρόσθ᾽ ἵππων 'in front of the horses'. Now while Nestor is occupied with detaching the horse from its harness, Hector, who has mounted his chariot for pursuit, approaches, 87ff. So the horse had only just been hit, probably at the moment when the chariot driver had approached to pick up Nestor for flight. (Incidentally, it is mentioned in other passages as well that the horses are positioned immediately behind the fighting heroes with their heads turned towards the enemy, e. g. N 385, P 502.) Diomedes and Nestor in their turn make at the enemy who are advancing in triumph, but Zeus hinders their bold enterprise with his thunder-bolt, and Hector continues his pursuit by chariot (Θ 184) of the wildly fleeing Achaeans, who crowd in confusion into the ditch, 214. It suits this situation exactly when in 254, in the rally which Zeus suddenly brings about, Diomedes and the Greek leaders turn their chariots against the Trojans, and Trojan leaders are hit from the chariots while fleeing, 258; this is merely the reverse of the immediately preceding picture. In the battle which follows, 261ff., the Greek heroes – at least Teucer, Ajax and Agamemnon – appear on foot; Hector on the other hand is still standing on his chariot, perhaps because he was just returning to battle from flight (cf. 313 Ἕκτορος ἡνιοχῆα ἱέμενον πολέμονδε βάλε 'he hit Hector's charioteer as he was charging into battle'), but now jumps down, 320, to take revenge on

Teucer for shooting his driver; the wounded Teucer is then carried out of the battle, 334. Then, according to the Olympian's will, Hector, at the head of the Trojans, throws the Greeks back across the ditch and, when they have crossed, he drives up and down on the edge of the ditch, **[I.20]** evidently an example of what the leaders were generally doing, 'to kill any individuals who might have stayed on the near side of the ditch' (Ameis). Night then interrupts the victorious run of the Trojans, 485-6, and Hector leads his men back to the Scamander, during which all who have a chariot naturally use it. Only when the order is given to 'Halt!' do they dismount in order to listen to Hector's words in the assembly, 492.

At Λ 178ff., on the third battle-day, the Trojans flee, chased by Agamemnon, until at Iris' instigation the flight comes to a halt; then Hector jumps off his chariot, 211, moves quickly along the whole army, sets his forces in order again, and the battle restarts. At Λ 284ff., after Agamemnon has been wounded, a general flight has broken out among the Achaeans. Some of the pursuing Trojans appear on their chariots, 289, while Diomedes and Odysseus, the two Greek heroes who are still trying to stop the pursuers, fight on foot, even against the Trojans who are attacking by chariot, 320, 328, 423. Ajax fights on foot as well, 545, and so does Hector in 336-68 (undoubtedly in my view an interpolation),[8] until he is hit violently on the helmet by Diomedes and pulls back, 354; when he has regained consciousness, he immediately mounts his chariot, 360, and ἐξέλασ᾽ ἐς πληθύν 'drove off into the crowd' to get to a different part of the battle-field; in 498ff. he appears μάχης ἐπ᾽ ἀριστερὰ ... πάσης ... μέρμερα ῥέζων ἔγχεῖ θ᾽ ἱπποσύνῃ τε 'on the far ... left ... creating havoc with spear and chariot'. When Cebriones, who is standing next to him 522, sees how the Trojans, pressed hard by Ajax, retreat in wild flight, 525 Τρῶες ὀρίνονται ἐπιμίξ, ἵπποι τε καὶ αὐτοί 'the Trojans are running off in chaos, chariots and all', Hector drives across the battle field, 533, to help his hard-pressed comrades, for he ἵετο δῦναι ὅμιλον ἀνδρόμεον ῥῆξαί τε μετάλμενος, 537 'was eager to get in among the throng of fighting men, to charge and break through', and, fighting on foot, 540, performs splendid deeds.

The chariot is, of course, regularly used to drive back the wounded hero from battle. Thus Agamemnon, who was not wounded seriously, jumps on to his chariot, Λ 273-4, 280-1; so does Diomedes, 399 ἐς δίφρον δ᾽ ἀνόρουσε 'he sprang into his chariot' to be driven back to the ships, and Menelaus leads the wounded Odysseus from the tumult, 488, until the chariot driver arrives with the chariot. Machaon, although he is called ποιμὴν λαῶν, 506 'shepherd of the people', and had brought the κρατεραὶ στίχες ἀσπιστάων λαῶν ... Τρίκης ἐξ ἱπποβότοιο 'the powerful shield-bearing force ... from Tricce *where the horses graze*' to Troy, Δ 202, still did not fight from a chariot; so when he is wounded Idomeneus asks Nestor to drive him to the ships on his chariot. The horseman Nestor, Λ 516, who must likewise have been present in the battle on foot, mounts his chariot therefore and drives with the doctor to the camp. Eurypylos, 842 ποιμένα λαῶν 'shepherd of the people' did not fare so well. Since he had no chariot, he had to drag himself to the ships on foot, however hard this was for him, 811.

To make possible the instant use of the chariot even during the battle, the choice of chariot driver was obviously of the greatest importance. He always had to stay close to his commander with the horses, and often had to display more courage and spirit than the best fighter, so that his commander would not fare like Agastrophus who, wounded by Diomedes, was unable to flee, Λ 340, because his horses were not nearby, τοὺς μὲν γὰρ θεράπων ἀπάνευθ' ἔχεν 'his charioteer was holding the horses some way off'. The moment in particular when the general rout was beginning and everyone started to run for it while the enemy pressed forward, made the highest demands on his loyalty, reliability and skill. This was because, in spite of the general confusion, he had to drive up to his commander, often enough against the stream of men, or wait for him until he had mounted. This moment was particularly favourable for the victor to kill a leading opponent and because of this it frequently happens in the epic that a hero is felled at the very moment when he is mounting the chariot to flee. The intimate relationship which thus existed between warrior and chariot driver **[I.21]** has been frequently pointed out, e. g. in Köpke p. 141ff., and the particular danger of the position of charioteer is shown by the many serious and fatal wounds which the epic describes as occurring among them. The conscientious fulfilling of their task was especially difficult when they had to deal with nervous horses, unwilling to stay in position or to obey their directions when close to the fighting. This happened to the worthy Cleitus, Ο 445ff., Polydamas' chariot driver, who πεπόνητο καθ' ἵππους 'was having difficulty with his horses', because he always tried to keep them close by in the densest confusion of battle, 448, and fell, hit by an arrow of Teucer's ὄπισθε 'from behind' – as Faesi attractively explains on 451 'since, through being occupied with the nervous horses, he could very well find himself in circumstances in which he turned his back to the enemy.' Polydamas therefore caught the horses himself and, before he rejoined the front line, 457, personally instructed Astynous, who took them over, σχεδὸν ἴσχειν ... ἵππους 'to keep the horses close at hand'.

It was precisely for this reason that Patroclus chose Automedon as his chariot driver, Π 147, because he could be absolutely confident that in battle he would μεῖναι ὁμοκλήν 'keep within calling distance' and thus, while he himself was fighting on foot, would be ready at any moment to pick him up if he shouted. After Patroclus' death, when Automedon has found Alcimedon ready to take over control of the horses while he himself wants to get down to fight, P 480 ἐγὼ δ' ἵππων ἀποβήσομαι, ὄφρα μάχωμαι 'I shall get down to fight', he orders him expressly to keep the horses in his immediate vicinity, 502 μάλ' ἐμπνείοντε μεταφρένῳ 'their breath on my back'. Again, the scene which features Antilochus' chariot driver Laodocus (who is mentioned only in passing) gives us some useful information about our question. Antilochus was found by Menelaus P 683, θαρσύνονθ' ἑτάρους καὶ ἐποτρύνοντα μάχεσθαι 'encouraging his troops and driving them on to fight'; Menelaus told him to leave the fighting and take the news of Patroclus' death quickly to Achilles, and Antilochus gave his armour Λαοδόκῳ, ὅς οἱ σχεδὸν ἔστρεφε μώνυχας ἵππους 'to Laodocus, who was manoeuvring his horses up and down beside him' P 699. The passage is indicative of the location of the chariot during battle. For if Antilochus can calmly take off weapons and armour and give them to the chariot driver, the latter really must be positioned behind the line of fighting men. This moreover was the only place where he could find the space to drive to and fro while his superior jumped forward, now to the right, now to the left, against an enemy in the σταδίη μάχη 'standing fight'. It likewise precludes the view that there was a whole row of chariots behind the front line, for then ἔστρεφε 'was manoeuvring' (imperfect) would have been impossible. The fact that, despite the extreme urgency of the message, 691ff., Antilochus takes off his armour and runs rather than using his horses (which admittedly were not the fastest)[9] could also be referred to as proof of the limited mobility of the chariots and so of their still more limited efficiency in battle, as compared with the foot soldiers.

The task of the chariot drivers turns out a little differently in passage M 76ff. which is equally important for our analysis. There, following Hector's example in accordance with Polydamas' advice, 61ff., the leaders had left their chariots, to form up as assault troops on the near side of the ditch and to cross it πεντάχα κοσμηθέντες 'organised ... in five contingents'. According to usual practice, the chariot drivers would now have had to follow behind their superiors who did not want to wait in the chariots until the battle began; or, perhaps, the commanders could have been driven for a distance beyond the ditch up to the wall, like the Greek leaders when they first came out. But with wise caution, Polydamas requires that the chariots should be left behind now and stay by the ditch, not so much because of the difficulty of the crossing, but rather because he feared the terrible confusion that would inevitably ensue if the attack was beaten off and the Achaeans made some kind of forward push, and then foot soldiers and chariots wanted to cross back over the ditch all at the same time. So the drivers receive the order, M 85, ἵππους εὖ κατὰ κόσμον ἐρυκέμεν **[I.22]** αὖθ᾽ ἐπὶ τάφρῳ 'to hold back their horses in good order there at the ditch'. That is why, at N 535, Polites had to help his wounded brother out of the battle up to the ditch where he found his chariot, 537; and also the wounded Hector is carried by his friends to the horses, Ξ 430, οἵ οἱ ὄπισθε μάχης ἠδὲ πτολέμοιο ἔστασαν, 'which were standing for him behind the fighting', and then driven to the Scamander.

Asius earlier, M 108ff., had not followed Polydamas' advice directed at the ἀγοί 'commanders', 61, but drove across the ditch with his chariot, 119ff. His men, however, fight only on foot, and Asius himself also appears as a foot soldier during the assault on the wall and during the battle (Faesi on M 137), just as in the later battle within the wall, N 385-6, he appears, admittedly with his chariot, but πεζὸς πρόσθ᾽ ἵππων 'on foot in front of his horses'.

The passage O 354ff. too is characteristic of the epic conception of the use of ἵπποι 'horses' in the battles of the *Iliad*. The Achaeans are in wild flight back to the ships; Hector, who has so far been fighting on foot, appears in his chariot for the pursuit, 352, and with him the Trojans, 354, πάντες ὁμοκλήσαντες ἔχον ἐρυσάρματας ἵππους 'to a man gave an answering shout and drove on their horses and chariots'. Apollo strides ahead to clear the way for them and, to remove any obstacle to the crossing, he tramples down the sides of the ditch, ὅσον τ᾽ ἐπὶ δουρὸς ἐρωὴ γίγνεται, 358 'wide as the distance a man throws a spear', i.e. to a breadth of about ten to fifteen paces. Now even if we assume this created a path twenty paces wide, it is still impossible for chariot squadrons to advance across such a space in an attack; at best it would be sufficient for a few leaders on their chariots. But of course the poet did not have any more than that in mind here.

Again, Patroclus and the Myrmidons, Π 278ff., appear in battle on foot. They have chased the Trojans from Protesilaus' ship, but the latter are not yet flying προτροπάδην 'in headlong rout' 304, but still resist as they retreat. As long as an actual battle is taking place, neither Greek nor Trojan leaders mount their chariots. But developments become less and less favourable to the Trojans; here and there a man mounts his chariot, and Meriones kills Acamas ἵππων ἐπιβησόμενον, 343 'as he was about to mount his chariot'. Hector, however, although he γίγνωσκε μάχης ἑτεραλκέα νίκην 362 'was well aware that the enemy's reinforcements had won them the day',[10] stays in the battle for a while longer and tries to cover the retreat, 363. Only when the Greeks are pressing closer and closer forward does he mount his chariot and abandon his men, 367, and then the other mounted men follow him in wild flight, 370, 375-6, as do the foot soldiers. Then Patroclus too appears on his chariot, 377ff., drives past the fleeing men and specifically chases after Hector, 382, without being able to catch him. In the ensuing bloodbath that he causes, he is on foot again, 398, 404, 411, but immediately afterwards he is chasing with his horses again after the fleeing Lycians, whose commander jumps off his chariot to face him in battle. When Patroclus sees his opponent is willing to fight, he too jumps to the ground, ready to take him on, 426-7.

At Π 647ff., after the fighting has been going on for some time, Zeus decides to grant Patroclus the glory of driving Hector and the Trojans right back to the city. First, therefore, he instils fear into Hector, who in 657 ἐς δίφρον δ᾽ ἀναβὰς φύγαδ᾽ ἔτραπε, κέκλετο δ᾽ ἄλλους Τρῶας φευγέμεναι 'leapt into his chariot and wheeled it round for flight, shouting to the other Trojans to take to their heels'. All the men flee with him and not even the Lycians resist any longer, 659, while Patroclus, who had fought against Sarpedon and for the latter's corpse on foot, now pursues them by chariot, 684-5. When Hector, to cover the Trojans' flight, obeys Apollo's instruction and drives at him 724, Patroclus jumps off his chariot, 733, and hurls a rock at Hector, with which he fatally wounds his chariot driver Cebriones. Furious, Hector now jumps down as well, 755, and a general battle develops over Cebriones' corpse in which, as in the battle at the end of the book, Hector, Patroclus and all the heroes appear on foot. When therefore Hector, Π 833, calls to the dying Patroclus that his, Hector's, ὠκέες ἵπποι ποσσὶν ὀρωρέχαται πολεμίζειν 'swift horses race into battle' to protect the Trojan women and children, and Ameis explains 'the horses also contribute to the battle inasmuch as their speed **[I.23]** is of essential importance for the chariot fighter's success', I can agree with this explanation only in so far as I see the specially important help the horses give by conveying Hector swiftly to a place which is particularly threatened (e.g. shortly before at 728), or that they could rapidly bring him to his opponent's heels during a pursuit.

The incidental mention of the chariot in P 130 is perfectly in agreement with the view put forward so far. Hector, at the head of the Trojans, 107, had driven Menelaus away from Patroclus' corpse and removed its armour. But when Ajax approaches, Hector retreats in terror ἐς ὅμιλον ... ἑταίρων, 129 'into the crowd of his comrades' and the poet gives this fear an even more pointed expression through the addition ἐς δίφρον δ᾽ ἀνόρουσε 'and leapt onto his chariot'. Since Hector first retreated ἐς ὅμιλον 'into the crowd' and then mounted, the chariot naturally must have stood behind the line. Admittedly, what he does on the chariot is not expressly indicated; but that he did not mount it in order to fight, and that mounting the chariot during battle was not a sign of courage, is clearly shown by Glaucus when he reproaches Hector and calls him, 143, a φύξηλιν 'coward' because of this action. He also immediately afterwards appears on foot again to give the lie to Glaucus, 189-90, and again in the violent conflict which follows.

Reference to the ἵπποι 'horses' in P 740 ὡς μὲν τοῖς ἵππων τε καὶ ἀνδρῶν αἰχμητάων … ὀρυμαγδὸς ἐπήϊεν 'so the incessant din from fighting men and horses followed them' and Σ 153 αὖτις γὰρ δὴ τόν γε κίχον λαός τε καὶ ἵπποι 'the infantry and chariots caught up with it again' is kept so general that they can be understood as squadrons just as well as individual mounted men or the unoccupied chariots of the leaders. I, of course, take the last view and see confirmation of it for Σ 153 in the fact that in Homer the word λαός 'people' is normally used in the contrast between subordinates and their superiors, a contrast which here, too, I find in the addition of ἵπποι 'horses' and which is perhaps more accurate than the one I assumed in the *Lexicon Homericum* between λαός 'people' as *pedites* 'infantry' and ἵπποι 'horses' as *equites* 'mounted troops'. In the passage Σ 222, which has often been questioned (cf. Hentze, *App. Σ,* Intr. p. 119) where, startled by the voice and appearance of Achilles, the καλλίτριχες ἵπποι ἂψ ὄχεα τρόπεον 'the lovely-maned horses began to pull their chariots round', the ἡνίοχοι δ᾽ ἔκπληγεν 'and the charioteers were dumbfounded', I likewise interpret the ἵπποι 'horses' as being the empty chariots of the leaders and nobles following on behind, which all of a sudden turn round because they have a foreboding of disaster and because the chariot drivers have lost their heads in terror, as happens at N 394ff.; that is, they turn round without waiting for their commanders. Since this is repeated three times, 228, the drivers have each time turned again in between, so that it is quite understandable that a frightful confusion progressively builds up and that twelve φῶτες ἄριστοι 'distinguished men' are killed in the chaos, 230, by falling out or getting under the wheels or impaling themselves on their own spears, as they try to mount the chariots with the horses out of control. They are φῶτες ἄριστοι 'distinguished men' because only they own a chariot.

The reference to ἵπποι 'horses' in Υ 394 could seem surprising. On Apollo's instructions Hector has withdrawn from the front lines of fighters, 376, and Achilles, hurling himself at the Trojans, 381, rages devastatingly in their ranks. First he kills Iphition, ἰθὺς μεμαῶτα 'as this man came on against him', and loudly exults at slaying this dangerous opponent. Then we read 394, τὸν μὲν Ἀχαιῶν ἵπποι ἐπισσώτροις δατέοντο πρώτη ἐν ὑσμίνῃ 'The wheel-rims of the Greek chariot(s) tore him to pieces at the front of the fighting'. There is no reference to a general pursuit during which the Achaeans have mounted their chariots, and it is of course also improbable that whole squadrons should drive off over the corpse. It is probably Achilles' chariot which is meant here, since it was being driven to follow the hero and at 490ff. also was immediately at hand. On the other hand, it is entirely natural that the Trojans, terrified by Achilles' slaughter, think of immediate flight and mount their chariots; and it fits the situation very precisely when immediately afterwards, Y 401, Achilles kills Hippodamas καθ' ἵππων ἀίξαντα who 'had leapt from his chariot'. Here I agree with the explanation given by Faesi: 'He probably got down because the chariot which was **[I.24]** facing the enemy could not be turned round quickly enough, and salvation by flight seemed to him more possible this way'. After the brief duel with Hector, 419ff., Achilles slaughters the Trojans *en masse* during their headlong flight; the sons of Bias ἄμφω ... ἐξ ἵππων ὦσε χαμᾶζε, 461 'he dashed them both from their chariot to the ground', and (among many whom he kills on foot) Rhigmus on his chariot, 487. The latter had evidently tried to oppose him, for Achilles hit him in the stomach; on the other hand, he hit his chariot driver, who had swiftly turned the horses, in the back, 488. Then we see him himself on his chariot driving through the terrified Trojans and separating them from each other, Φ 3, so that half of them are chased into the river in total confusion, ἐπιμὶξ ἵππων τε καὶ ἀνδρῶν, Φ 16 'a medley of men and horses'. In the river, as in all the following fights, Achilles appears on foot and the chariot is never mentioned; however, after Hector's death, the chariot is immediately at hand again, X 398.

I hope that the passages discussed can be regarded as sufficient to justify the preceding sketch of the use of chariots and to provide a secure basis for the discussion in the following sections. Although various matters still remain to be explained, restricted space and concern about monotony prevent me from citing even more passages. I shall occasionally have to come to particular points later on.

Let us now follow the army which, after the marshalling has been completed and after exhortation and instruction from the leaders, advances into battle from the mustering-place.

Advance into Battle

In the epic this action, which naturally did not offer as much diversity and variety as the battle itself, is described in detail only once, on the first battle-day. There is no reference anywhere to a signal for the simultaneous advance of the whole line, given, as it might be, by the commander in chief. In this respect too the complete independence of the individual tribal leaders appears to be respected, cf. Δ 427: ἐπασσύτεραι Δαναῶν κίνυντο φάλαγγες νωλεμέως πολέμονδε, κέλευε δὲ οἷσιν ἔκαστος ἡγεμόνων 'one after the other, the Greek contingents moved relentlessly into battle. Each leader was issuing orders to his own command'. Agamemnon during his ἐπιπώλησις 'tour of inspection' immediately before the beginning of the battle finds the individual tribes in quite different states of readiness: Δ 232 καί ῥ'οὓς μὲν σπεύδοντας ἴδοι ... θαρσύνεσκε 'any that he found up and doing, he encouraged them'; 240 οὕστινας αὖ μεθιέντας ἴδοι ... νεικείεσκε 'if he found any hanging back ... he turned on them angrily'. The Cretans are already advancing 251ff.; so are the troops of the two Ajaxes 281ff.; Nestor too has finished his drawing up and is giving final instructions to his men 294ff.; but Menestheus with the Athenians and close by him Odysseus with the Cephallenians had not yet heard the battle cry, 331, with which men fighting elsewhere had already begun the conflict, but rather the contingents on both sides at this point were just starting to move, 332ff.

I interpret Δ 334ff. slightly differently from the commentators known to me. It is said there of the Athenian and Cephallenian troops: οἱ δὲ μένοντες ἕστασαν, ὁππότε πύργος Ἀχαιῶν ἄλλος ἐπελθὼν Τρώων ὁρμήσειε καὶ ἄρξειαν πολέμοιο 'they stood there waiting for some other Greek contingent to advance against the Trojans and would then start fighting'. I regard the verb ὁρμήσειε 'advance' as the predicate of πύργος 'contingent' but ἄρξειαν 'start' as predicate of οἱ δὲ μένοντες 'they, waiting' and interpret: they were not yet in the process of advancing, but were standing there, ready to strike, waiting for another πύργος Ἀχαιῶν 'Greek contingent' i.e. a company **[I.25]** in close order, to join them to set off against the Trojans and would then start the fighting together with this πύργος 'contingent'. Düntzer who only notes 'καί = and then' on this passage, seems to be of the same opinion, whereas Faesi, Ameis and La Roche refer ἄρξειαν 'start' to πύργος 'contingent' and the former two consequently add 'the Cephallenians and Athenians wanted to participate in the battle only in the second phase'. But the assumption of a second phase, a second line, does not find support either in our passage or in any others. The reason for waiting seems to me to lie merely in the fact that, all along the line, the battle develops in sections, and this is only now happening here. One could imagine the course of events in this way: where Pandarus' arrow was shot, the men seized their weapons first, and the advance gradually spread with the battle cry, in which case one has of course dropped the assumption that the whole army had seen the shot. This is why Agamemnon says to them 340: 'Why are you standing about, waiting for others? You should be the first to start the battle; but now you would perhaps still watch contentedly and idly even if ten πύργοι 'contingents' were involved in the battle before you.' The poet does not make Odysseus think even remotely about going ahead in a 'second phase'; and besides, there was no occasion for such an assumption in the whole situation. This is shown by the resolute answer of Odysseus, who describes the whole speech of Agamemnon as ἀνεμώλια βάζειν, 355 'hot air' because (he says) when battle with the Trojans begins he always fights with his opponent in the front line. Diomedes too, whom we have to imagine being on the wing of the total formation, was found by Agamemnon, 365, not yet participating in the battle (as we saw above); he jumps off his chariot only after Agamemnon's words, and since both armies are standing very close to each other, battle soon flares up all along the line. Again, in Y 329 the Caucones were still busy with their preparations, although in other places the battle had already been raging for a long time.

During the advance to battle by the first contingents, which took place immediately after the drawing up, Γ 2ff., and before the armies were standing as close to each other as they were when Pandarus shot his arrow, it was emphasised as an essential difference between the Greeks and Trojans that the Trojans κλαγγῇ τ᾽ ἐνοπῇ τ᾽ ἴσαν, ὄρνιθες ὥς, ἠΰτε περ κλαγγὴ γεράνων πέλει οὐρανόθι πρό, κ. τ. λ. 'advanced with shrieks and cries, like birds; as is the screaming of cranes beneath the skies, etc.' whereas the Achaeans, 8, advanced σιγῇ μένεα πνείοντες ... ἐν θυμῷ μεμαῶτες ἀλεξέμεν ἀλλήλοισιν 'in silence, breathing courage ... filled with determination to stand by one another'. This contrast between the two armies is taken up again in Δ 429ff. and expressed still more pointedly. Now it cannot possibly have been the poet's intention here to assert that the Trojans hurled themselves into battle with a battle-cry, whereas the Greeks maintained utter silence, since in other passages, indeed most of the time, this natural expression of courage is expressly mentioned for both sides, while here something which specifically disparages the Trojans must be expressed. It seems to me that one needs to distinguish sharply and precisely between silence during the advance into battle after the drawing up, during which only the words of command of the leaders ought to be heard, Δ 428-31, and the battle-cry which immediately precedes the attack, the beginning of battle. Since we should not imagine the mustering-places on both sides to be too close to each other, the advance (from the drawing up to the first clash) could in reality take rather a long time, and it is precisely in this that the discipline of the Greek troops shows itself, in contrast to the Trojans, that they keep quiet in the ranks: ἀκὴν ἴσαν, οὐδέ κε φαίης τόσσον λαὸν ἕπεσθαι ἔχοντ᾽ ἐν στήθεσιν αὐδήν, σιγῇ, δειδιότες σημάντορας 'the men advanced in silence. You would not think so large an army was on the march or had a voice, so silent were they, in fear of their commanders'. But the Trojans chatter and make a noise like cranes ready to take wing or a flock of unmilked sheep. In any case, the battle-cry sounds quite different from the bleating of **[I.26]** sheep, in spite of the different languages among the Trojans and their allies, and the word ἀλαλητός, 'hubbub', which is used here, 436: ὡς Τρώων ἀλαλητὸς ἀνὰ στρατὸν εὐρὺν ὀρώρει 'so a hubbub went up through the great army of the Trojans' does not refer to a battle-cry at all but, as usual, to a tumultuous din, cf. e.g. B 149 where it is said quite similarly: τοὶ δ’ ἀλαλητῷ νῆας ἔπ’ ἐσσεύοντο 'They rushed with cries for the ships', or Σ 149 where we are told about the Achaeans θεσπεσίῳ ἀλαλητῷ ὑφ’ Ἕκτορος ... φεύγοντες *'running* with *cries of terror* from Hector'. And how absurd it would be to assume that, if the Trojans' behaviour is supposed to be typical here, they must have shouted all the time during the advance, i.e. from drawing up until contact with their enemy. With all this shouting, the troops would have come to their enemy breathless and utterly exhausted. Just as little is it typical of the Greeks, that they do not raise the battle cry, as we shall repeatedly see. No, we find here in established practice the first traces of what was later praised in the Dorians, that they advanced in close order in complete silence, so that commands from the generals were quietly passed on by the junior officers to the men. The Greeks march silently, as is proper for regular soldiers, while the barbarians cannot keep their mouths shut and all chatter at once in different languages. The battle-cry comes only later, and Δ 331, already mentioned above, shows that it should not be excluded in this situation also: οὐ γάρ πώ σφιν ἀκούετο λαὸς ἀϋτῆς 'The battle-cry had not yet reached their ears'.

But this advance in complete silence presupposes good discipline and is possible only if it takes place in good order and fairly closed formation, as we have assumed. This by no means removes from the Dorians the distinction of having invented the attack in a closed line (cf. Duncker, op. cit., III p. 376, Thuc. V 70), since only with the music which they introduced does it become possible to march in step, and only a line which is marching in step can keep up a closed front for any length of time. Of course one should not imagine the whole army in close formation, since the tribes did not even advance simultaneously, and gradually considerable gaps must have opened between the individual contingents, through which a chariot driver (for instance) could easily advance ahead of the front line to reach his commander and the latter for his part could get to his chariot driver, or individual heroes could leave the battle line because they were wounded or wanted to get new weapons.

It goes without saying that the advance is made at walking speed so as not to exhaust the men's strength too early and disorder the lines, even if Herodotus, VI 112, did not expressly assure us that at Marathon an attack was made by the Greeks at the double for the first time. Marching in line requires that spears are held high, perhaps carried over the shoulder, and this is probably supposed to be implied by the expression, Δ 281, πυκιναὶ κίνυντο φάλαγγες ... σάκεσίν τε καὶ ἔγχεσι πεφρικυῖαι 'the close-packed ranks moved off ... *bristling with* shields and *spears*'.

The best heroes are to be found in the front line, but we repeatedly find the leader out in front of his contingent, something which appears as vain ostentation in Paris, Γ 16ff., because the armies had not yet come within range of each other and he, armed only with bow and sword, could not anyway have taken up the fight against an Achaean hero to which he is making a challenge. That is how the two Ajaxes marched into battle in front of their men, Δ 274, Hector Ł 592, N 136, O 306, P 107, 262, Poseidon in front of the Greeks, Ξ 384, always, of course, on foot, and it is the leader who likes to hurl the first spear into the enemy lines and kill the first opponent. If the two armies clash, then naturally he steps back into the first line and, in general, even when he does not follow in his chariot, he **[I.27]** is in no way limited to this position during an advance. Thus it says of Idomeneus in Δ 253-4 ἐνὶ προμάχοις 'among the front fighters', of Meriones πυμάτας ὄτρυνε φάλαγγας 'he urged on the troops at the rear', i.e. the former was spurring on the warriors to fight in the front line, the latter in the rear lines.

The Standing Fight[11]

During battle on open ground, which the epic describes to us in its different phases with multiple variation of colourful individual pictures, as the fortunes of war turn out, two different kinds of battle must be distinguished which between them constitute the components of each battle-day. These are: the 'standing fight', during which the entire armies on both sides stand facing each other at some distance, ready to strike, but during which it is always only individual warriors or relatively small groups who fight in the space between; and the attack of a larger mass directed at the enemy line in close formation, which aims to force a breakthrough or drive the enemy back. In many respects the relationship to each other of the two kinds of battle is like that of firing in line and a charge with bayonets in modern warfare.

Only breaking through the enemy lines with a violent assault in a massed formation brings a certain and swift decision, which is the purpose and objective of any battle. The 'standing fight' can be regarded only as a preliminary to an attack, or as a pause between several consecutive attempts at an attack. The attempt at a breakthrough will in reality always take a relatively short time; during the bloody struggle, eye to eye with the enemy, it must very soon become apparent whether the assault can be carried through, i.e. whether the enemy line is being broken and is giving way, or whether the enemy's power of resistance has been underestimated. The successful breakthrough is followed by flight and pursuit on foot; if the attempt has been repelled, then a 'standing fight' ensues in order to regroup one's forces, or it becomes necessary to repel an attack by the enemy. Often the intended push is not in fact carried through. The opponents wait for the advancing enemy in an orderly, massed formation, but the latter approaches only up to a short distance and offers only a 'standing fight' until circumstances appear more favourable. Again, the opponent who has been defeated and is in flight, if he receives some unexpected help, can, at the command of a god or a brave leader, recover and regroup and thus give the pursuer a reason on his part to bring his scattered contingents into formation again and begin a 'standing fight' afresh, to make or resist an attack. In any case, the two types of battle are most closely connected with each other, develop from each other, take place not only one after the other but also simultaneously at different parts of the battle line – e.g. in P 354–65 a battle in massed formation is described, while at the same time, 370ff., a 'standing fight' takes place – but it is always the case that in the descriptions of epic, as in real life, the 'standing fight' constitutes the basic situation out of which individual attacks develop, pushing forward in different places and very frequently returning to the line.

But before I pass on to a discussion of the poet's passages which are to explain and confirm the brief sketch above, I must say a word in advance about **[I.28]** the use which should, in my opinion, be made of the pictures of fighting and battle given in the epic for answering our question. In particular passages of his battle descriptions, Homer has his eye on great numbers, e.g. when he talks about their advance, at which the ground shakes and enormous dust clouds darken the sun; or when he has the opposing armies clashing like two mountain torrents which pour into a single gorge; or when he repeatedly emphasises that intense danger threatens the Achaeans or the Trojans in the battle, or when he has the men falling to the ground under the hail of missiles. But in the actual descriptions he picks out only individual scenes; he does not describe the battle to us as it rages along the whole line, but only as it develops at individual points of it. He does, of course, occasionally take us to another part of the battlefield, but without indicating through more than a brief hint that the action at the various points serves one great common purpose. He does not describe the brave deeds of tribes or whole armies, but almost exclusively of individual heroes. But when in the evening of the battle-day he has the battlefield littered with corpses, Θ 491 ἀγορὴν ποιήσατο ... Ἕκτωρ ἐν καθαρῷ, ὅθι δὴ νεκύων διεφαίνετο χῶρος 'Hector summoned a meeting ... in an open space where the ground was clear of bodies', cf. K 199, 349, (the vile activity of corpse strippers appears to be already familiar, K 343), and has Diomedes stride away with Odysseus through armour and dark blood K 298, when the ground runs with blood Δ 451, and many Trojans and Achaeans lie next to each other stretched out in the dust Δ 544, then we know that there were not only

54

individual heroes fighting at individual points, while the others comfortably watched, but that whole masses have faced each other in battle; we know that, with his individual descriptions, the poet gives us only individual figures from the total picture, as examples so to speak, designed to illustrate the whole course of a battle.[12] Duels certainly occur as well, during which the whole army looks on; and the challenging by name of an individual opponent in the 'standing fight', which is very appropriate to this type of fighting, could certainly give many a brave hero the opportunity brilliantly to display his competence and his courage against a particularly dangerous opponent. But real success is not achieved by killing a single opponent, however capable he may be, but by the forced flight of the entire enemy army. Obviously, for the attainment of this goal, the bravery of the outstanding individual hero has a quite different significance from the battles of later times; but one should not forget that according to the view presented in the whole epic – which is what one would expect in an already highly developed culture – war is regarded as a serious matter, felt as a heavy burden, which is endured only out of urgent necessity, but whose speedy conclusion is striven for with all one's might, not as a noble sport for individual heroes, that the annihilation of the enemy is the purpose of battle, and that all means which serve this purpose are allowed and right – one would not, for example, have a crisis of conscience about the use of the λόχος 'ambush'.

It is self-evident that in the unlimited appreciation of the effect of outstanding heroic valour the poet is using his imagination – quite justifiably – when an individual hero like Achilles puts whole armies to flight. Myth has then made the hero into a champion of his whole race; but that skill could not be taught in the tactics of the heroic age, and we must not regard such an occurrence as drawn from the mundane reality of the battlefield. All the same, from the numerous individual incidents and descriptions which the poet so vividly presents to us, I think that we may construct for ourselves a general picture of the whole progress of a battle at that time. **[I.29]** The very first battle scenes described in the epic can serve this purpose.

After Pandarus' shot, both armies have advanced against each other. After a short clash which has evidently been indecisive (for only such a clash can be described in verses Δ 446-56), the armies are now in the middle of a 'standing fight'. Ajax has fatally hit Simoeisius πρῶτον ἰόντα, 480 'as he advanced among the front ranks'; in reply Priam's son Antiphus throws at him καθ' ὅμιλον 'through the crowd'. He misses Ajax and hits Leucus, who is dragging the corpse across to the Greek side, 492, and is thus standing next to Ajax. Now, furious at his friend's death – the battle-order assumed above at the drawing up of the contingents has been dropped completely for the individual scenes

– Odysseus advances through the πρόμαχοι 'front ranks', 495, comes up very close to the Trojans and brandishes his spear for a deadly throw, keeping a watch around him on both sides. But the Trojans, fearful of an imminent cast from a sure hand at close quarters, press back nervously, and the whole line of the πρόμαχοι 'front ranks' together with Hector retreats some way from the impact of the spear, 505, leaving Democoon, Odysseus' victim, lying there. The Achaeans seize this favourable moment to make a rapid push, and with loud cheering drag the corpses of Simoeisius, Democoon and Leucus across to their side.

The poet uses a very similar method in Π 582ff. to describe the vigorous, formidable advance of Patroclus: his stone-throw breaks Sthenelaus' neck and the πρόμαχοι 'front ranks' together with Hector retreat the length of a spear-throw; the Achaeans immediately charge after them until Glaucus suddenly turns and brings down the first Achaean who had come too close to him. This recoil of a whole line from the missile of a feared opponent, hurled from a short distance with great accuracy, but naturally only so far as it is threatened by the spear-throw, is frequently mentioned by the poet and certainly taken from the live course of a battle; but it is not an indication of any particular cowardice but rather of a natural loss of nerve, which gives an advantage to the menacing enemy, when he might have been fore-stalled by a throw from the opposing line. All the same it is a danger-ous moment, since such a recoil can easily be turned into an effective advance by the opponent, as is the case at Π 593. This leads to Apollo's immediate intervention in our passage when, incensed by the slack-ness of the Trojans, Δ 507, he urgently shouts at them not to give way.

The victor however does not always succeed in taking advantage of this moment to strip his fallen opponent. In Ο 573 Antilochus, just like Odysseus here, had leapt forward from the front line of fighters and from close range made a deadly throw into the Trojan ranks at Melanippus, from which the nearby Trojans had backed away in fear. But when he wants to use this moment to snatch the armour, 583, Hector leaps out at him and Antilochus quickly runs away from him, without turning round until he reaches the company of his comrades. When they see this, the other Trojans quickly pluck up courage and with loud shouts launch a hail of missiles at the man in flight, but – and this has certainly also been taken from life – not a single one of them hits him.

While Apollo encourages the Trojans, Athene makes her way along the lines of the Greeks, Δ 516 αὐτὰρ Ἀχαιοὺς ὦρσε Διὸς θυγάτηρ ... ἐρχομένη καθ' ὅμιλον, ὅθι μεθιέντας ἴδοιτο 'The Greeks were encouraged by the daughter of Zeus ... who went through the ranks spurring on any she saw holding back'. μεθιέναι 'hold back' in this type of battle (in

which only individual warriors or smaller groups participate) probably means that the warriors in question, protected behind their
shields, **[I.30]** calmly remain in their places without throwing their
weapons into the enemy line or at individual opponents who have
leapt forward, or without themselves advancing for a sure throw, during which they could, of course, easily give their opponent a target
which was often effectively exploited. Now Diores, hit by a stone
thrown by the Thracian leader Peirous, sinks into the dust and
stretches out his hands to his comrades, imploring their help, 523.
The Thracian boldly leaps out at him to deal the death-blow and dart
back again. He succeeds in doing the one, but as he turns back after
the spear thrust, Thoas wounds him with his spear and kills him with
his sword. But when Thoas tries to take away his armour as well, the
Thracians advance and hold their long spears lowered over the corpse
so that Thoas has to withdraw, and both corpses stay lying there
between the armies. Further bloody battles arise over their possession, 538, 543-4.

After the mighty deeds which the poet has had Diomedes perform in
his *aristeia* under the protection of the august war goddess herself,
the poet presents us with the picture of a 'standing fight' again in Ε
494ff. The Trojans had turned around from their flight, regrouped and
now attack the Achaeans who in the meantime have likewise re-
formed their ranks. The Danaans stand firm and Agamemnon with
his spear hits Deicoön who is standing in the front line next to
Aeneas, 534. Aeneas immediately leaps forward and kills the two sons
of Diocles, 541; incensed by this, Menelaus moves against him out of
the line of front fighters, 562, blinded by Ares who wants him to be
killed by Aeneas. Antilochus sees the dangerous advance of the king,
also goes διὰ προμάχων 'through the front ranks' and stands by his
side; but when Aeneas sees the two heroes next to each other and
ready to fight, 572, he hastily withdraws, so that they can now easily
drag the dead Achaeans back to their side, μετὰ λαὸν 'Αχαιῶν, 573
'into the Achaean army'; then they turn and rejoin the fight μετὰ
πρώτοισι 'in the front ranks'. Menelaus brings Pylaemenes down with
his spear and Antilochus hits his chariot driver with a stone when he
is just about to turn the horses to flee; he drops the reins, and
Antilochus leaps on him and kills him with his sword. But now the
Trojans advance under Hector's leadership, and the Achaeans start to
retreat on Diomedes' instructions.

Ζ 84ff. As a result of Ajax's break-through of the Trojan lines, Ζ 6, a
general rout has been caused. On Helenus' advice Hector halts the
Trojans under the walls of the city and here they stand firm, fighting
despite their exhaustion until Hector and Paris return. Their re-
appearance, Η 1ff., and effective intervention in the fight have such a

stimulating effect on the Trojans that they even move from a 'standing fight' into an advance, which is at least partly successful. For the fact that Iphinous jumps on to his chariot, 15, marks the beginning of the defeat which is indicated even more clearly by verses 17ff. τοὺς ... ἐνόησεν ... Ἀθήνη Ἀργείους ὀλέκοντας ἐνὶ *κρατερῇ ὑσμίνῃ* 'Athene saw them *slaughtering the Greeks in the heat of battle*'. This, of course, did not bring about a decisive outcome to the day's fighting, and without such a decision the battle, which had already been raging for a long time, could not be broken off. When therefore Athene, who wishes for its end as much as Apollo, asks the latter in 36: ἀλλ' ἄγε, πῶς μέμονας πόλεμον καταπαυσέμεν ἀνδρῶν 'But come, how do you propose to stop the men from fighting?', he suggests bringing about the required decision through a duel. The fact that once again Hector on his own succeeds in pushing back all the Trojans with his spear, H 55, is of course poetic embellishment, or else Homer omits the details, such as the sending of heralds. Equally, the fact that the battle day concludes with a duel just as it started with one merely serves to round things off poetically, and has nothing to do with questions of tactics.

[I.31] In Λ 211ff. the flight of the Trojans was halted by Hector on Iris' instructions. Both sides restore order in their lines, which had been disrupted by flight and pursuit, 215-16, and then turn against each other. On the Greek side, Agamemnon leaps out first, 217, and in the conflict kills Iphidamas who comes against him, 240. But when he tries to remove the latter's armour, Coon, the fallen man's brother, darts at him, stabs him in the arm before he is aware, then grabs Iphidamas by the foot and, covered by his shield, tries to drag the corpse away. But before the ἄριστοι 'best men', whom he has called over, come to help, 258, Agamemnon brings him down in spite of the wound in his arm. Then he mounts his chariot, and as a result of a vigorous Trojan attack under Hector, 294, a general flight of the Achaeans now begins. So in a single scene, the poet has moved from the flight of the Trojans, which he had been describing up till then, to their victorious advance and pursuit.

I will now pick out a few examples from books N and O which are particularly rich in descriptions of the σταδίη μάχη 'standing fight'. In N 361ff. Idomeneus leaps on the Trojans who are terrified at the advance of the grizzled hero;[13] he fatally wounds Othryoneus with his spear, 370; but when he tries to drag him away by the foot, Asius comes to help and a scene develops which is quite similar to the one discussed above, Ŀ 580-9. Asius, standing in front of his chariot, is killed by Idomeneus, Antilochus leaps in and hits the chariot driver who falls from the chariot, and the victors drive the horses over to their side as booty. Then Idomeneus challenges Deiphobus, 448, but a fight does not ensue; rather they both call together their friends for help, 488ff., and a whole group of leaders and men advance against each other τιτυσκομένων καθ᾽ ὅμιλον ἀλλήλων, 499 'aiming at each other across the ranks'. In the course of this Aeneas aims at Idomeneus who, however, ἄντα ἰδὼν ἡλεύατο χάλκεον ἔγχος, 503 'was on the look-out and avoided his bronze spear'; then Idomeneus himself hits Oenomaus, from whose corpse he does manage to pull his spear; but he cannot take any of the armour as booty, because a shower of missiles is hurled at him when he leaps forward again for this purpose. The old warrior was simply no longer as nimble and quick at exploiting all the opportunities in the σταδίη μάχη 'standing fight', and from the poet's description of his deficiencies (512-16) we see what attributes were necessary for a good fighter in the σταδίη μάχη 'standing fight'. There it is said of him:

οὐ γὰρ ἔτ᾽ ἔμπεδα γυῖα ποδῶν ἦν ὁρμηθέντι,
οὔτ᾽ ἄρ᾽ ἐπαΐξαι μεθ᾽ ἑὸν βέλος οὔτ᾽ ἀλέασθαι.

'He was no longer quick enough to dash in and recover his own throw or avoid someone else's.' So Idomeneus was no longer fast enough for ὁρμᾶσθαι 'dashing in'; he could no longer nimbly leap after the missile he had hurled, 513, in order to use the enemy's confusion at its impact to seize not only his own weapon but a piece of booty as well; nor could he quickly ἀλέασθαι 'avoid a throw'. This probably does not merely mean, as Ameis wants, 'to evade enemy missiles with a leap to one side', since above, 503, the poet said of him ἄντα ἰδὼν ἡλεύατο χάλκεον ἔγχος 'was on the look-out and avoided his bronze spear'; but primarily it means, (in contrast to ἐπαΐξαι), to be quick enough, after leaping forward, to dash back with a piece of booty before the enemy plucked up courage and hurled their missiles. Therefore it is said further of him τῷ ῥα καὶ ἐν σταδίῃ μὲν ἀμύνετο νηλεὲς ἦμαρ 'so in the "standing fight" he kept off the pitiless day of death' – which could happen through skilful handling of the shield, which Hector boasts of in his own case at H 238, or by crouching behind the shield, as he had himself done already above 408, by κλίνεσθαι 'swerving', as Hector did H 254, or by ducking, as Meriones did in Π 610, cf. P 527. On the other hand, Idomeneus could no longer run back quickly, **[I.32]** τρέσσαι δ᾽ οὐκέτι ῥίμφα πόδες φέρον ἐκ πολέμοιο, 515, 'being too slow on his feet to save his life by running', so he went back step by step, 516 βάδην ἀπιόντος 'as he moved slowly off', his face of course turned towards the enemy.

So the main skill, apart from accurate throwing, consisted in lightning-quick leaping forwards and backwards, during which it was important all the time to keep one's eyes open in all directions in order not to miss the chance to regain one's own spear and a piece of booty from the enemy, or promptly to evade the oncoming enemy missile. Deiphobus had thrown at the retreating Idomeneus, but killed Ascalaphus, 520; he now quickly follows up his spear and tears off Ascalaphus' helmet; but, quick as Ares, 528, Meriones leaps forward, throws and strikes him, already retreating, in the arm with his spear so that he drops the captured helmet. With a second swoop Meriones seizes his spear, pulls it out of his enemy's arm, and ἄψ ἑτάρων ἐς ἔθνος ἐχάζετο, 533 'retreated into his own contingent of comrades'; but the wounded Deiphobus is led out of the fighting to his chariot by his brother.

It is typical of fighting in the σταδίη μάχη 'standing fight' that the poet in N 559 has Antilochus considering ἤ τευ ἀκοντίσσαι, ἠὲ σχεδὸν ὁρμηθῆναι 'whether he should throw his spear at an opponent or lunge at close range'. The spear is either hurled from a distance, according to Rüstow's assumption of fifteen to twenty paces, and then the hero leaps after it in order to retrieve it; or it is very commonly used for a thrust, for which the fighter must of course leap at his opponent, as in 541 above and 562. This is particularly easy to do when the latter has carelessly turned round, like Thoon in 545 who pays for this carelessness with his life. Therefore the expression ἐπαΐσσειν 'leap in' is often found in connection with οὐτάζειν 'stab', and σχεδόν 'at close range' with οὔτασε 'he stabbed' and similar words. While Antilochus, 560, still undecided about his target, brandishes his spear, Adamas, now using the moment well, leaps in and thrusts hard at him with his spear; but Poseidon protects Antilochus so that the spear shatters on the shield, and before Adamas, quickly retreating, can reach his own contingent of comrades, Meriones in pursuit hurls his spear at him, hits him fatally, and with a second swoop safely retrieves the spear from the dead man's body. The course of events in N 645-55 is very similar – only here Meriones wounds the retreating Harpalion with an arrow shot. But when in Π 784 the poet has Patroclus leap forward three times and kill nine enemies each time, we may regard such success as poetic embellishment, ascribing unusual strength to the hero who is being particularly celebrated.

This leaping forwards and backwards, this dodging to the right and left, the crouching and ducking, are what Hector so typically boasts about in himself, H 241, οἶδα δ' ἐνὶ σταδίῃ δηΐῳ μέλπεσθαι Ἄρηι 'and in a "standing fight" I know the steps of the War-god's deadly dance'. This might well seem to the fearless, battle-hardened hero like a round dance, which young men would perform face to face with each other in peace time. What mattered was not merely practised steps, but also flexibility and suppleness of the upper body and rhythmical use of the arms – and the customary bowing was not lacking either when the enemy spear was whistling towards you. It is very expressive when Aeneas in Π 617, furious that Meriones had dodged his spear through skilful ducking, 611, πρόσσω γὰρ κατέκυψε, τὸ δέ ... δόρυ μακρὸν οὔδει ἐνισκίμφθη 'for he ducked. The long shaft stuck in the ground', mocks him: Μηριόνη, τάχα κέν σε, καὶ *ὀρχηστήν* περ ἐόντα, ἔγχος ἐμὸν κατέπαυσε διαμπερές, εἴ σ᾽ ἔβαλόν περ 'Meriones, *you may be a fine dancer*, but my spear would have stopped you for good and all, if only I'd hit you.' This is what Idomeneus, with genuine heroic humour, calls the intimate contact of the fighters in the front lines, N 291 προμάχων ὀαριστύν 'the intimacy of battle in the front line', to which the hero is mightily drawn, and it could well do a fighter particular honour if it was said of him that he was ἀγαθὸς ἐν σταδίη ὑσμίνη 'a good man in a "standing fight"'. This is said of Teucer N 314 and in addition he is **[I.33]** praised for his distinction τοξοσύνη 'as an archer', since the bow is of course not the weapon for the σταδίη μάχη 'standing fight' but rather the spear, with the sword next. But we already explained above that uniform weapons are not presupposed by the poet: so in N 576 he has Helenus first attack with the sword and then shoot with the bow in the σταδίη μάχη 'standing fight', which is of course quite feasible from the front line. Only the archer is not well protected against a spear throw, unless like Teucer, Θ 266ff., he is shooting from the protection of another man's shield. Meriones too, N 650, and Paris occasionally use the bow in battle. But we should envisage these archers as isolated figures in the ranks of fighters.

The matter is a little different with the Locrians, who were armed only with the bow and therefore, as mentioned, were not usable in the σταδίη μάχη 'standing fight'. The employment of these troops as described in the epic is very interesting because it gives us the first indication of the mutual support of differently armed groups which was beginning to appear at that time. For in N 701ff. we are told that the two Ajaxes were standing in battle not far from each other. The Telamonian had his men behind him, into whose ranks he could withdraw when he needed a short rest, but of the Locrians of Oileus' son it is said 716ff.:

> ... τόξοισιν καὶ ἐϋστρόφῳ οἶος ἀώτῳ ...
> ταρφέα βάλλοντες Τρώων *ῥήγνυντο φάλαγγας*.
> δή ῥα τόθ᾽ *οἱ μὲν πρόσθε* σὺν ἔντεσι δαιδαλέοισι
> μάρναντο Τρωσίν τε καὶ Ἕκτορι χαλκοκορυστῇ,
> οἱ δ᾽ ὄπιθεν *βάλλοντες* ἐλάνθανον· οὐδέ τι χάρμης
> Τρῶες μιμνήσκοντο· συνεκλόνεον γὰρ ὀιστοί.

'They relied on bows and slings of well-twisted wool ... and used them extensively to *break through the Trojan ranks*. So now, while the troops in their ornate armour engaged the Trojans and bronze-clad Hector *in the front line*, the Locrians kept shooting at them from well out of sight *in the rear*. The Trojans, thrown into confusion by the arrows, began to lose their will to fight.' So the Locrians, positioned behind the lines and thus protected, tried with much success, 722, to break through the enemy formations with their arrows, i.e. they prepared and supported from a greater distance (causing all the more trouble for the enemy) the attempt at breaking through the opposing lines, ῥήγνυντο φάλαγγας 'they broke through the lines', to bring about a decision, while the Telamonian's men were trying to achieve the same goal in the spear-fight in front of them. The poet of this passage, the connection of which with the whole description may justifiably be described as somewhat confused, really has in mind, as it seems to me, the use of two differently armed companies for mutual support. In the rest of the battle scenes of the *Iliad* there is no further mention of this anywhere, at least not again so clearly.

From the large number of other descriptions of the σταδίη μάχη 'standing fight' in the epic, I may be allowed to quote one or two individual features. The warrior who has leapt forward from his line, even if he does not retreat βάδην 'slowly' like Idomeneus, normally withdraws with his face towards the enemy. This explains why Hector, Ξ 412, when he is hurrying back into the company of his comrades after his shot at Ajax, is hit in the chest by Ajax, and Polydamas, 461, when Ajax καρπαλίμως ἀπιόντος ἀκόντισε 'quickly threw at him as he withdrew', can still dodge the missile just in time with a leap to the side, 463 λικριφὶς ἀΐξας 'by leaping to one side'. Antilochus, O 590, on the other hand had turned round when he was retreating from Hector in terror, and therefore the whole mass of Trojans hurled their missiles at him. This rapid leaping forwards and backwards (cf. also O 520, 525, 529, 571 ἐξάλμενος 'racing out'), which happens from different parts of the line on both sides, probably allows, *mutatis mutandis*, a comparison with the game of 'Prisoners' Base' played by our children. In addition to this there might occasionally occur a longer duel between two heroes **[I.34]** , as is reported of Dolops in O 539, the top of whose helmet Meges had hit with a spear, that he τῷ πολέμιζε μένων 'stood his ground and fought on against him'. But this was unlucky for him, for while he was paying attention solely to this opponent, Menelaus stepped forward from the line and brought him down from the side with his spear, 541.

In the type of fighting usual in the σταδίη μάχη 'standing fight' as described above, in which anybody could leap forward out of the line at will, in which sometimes a group would advance, sometimes retreat to quite a large distance, it is very understandable that the coherence of the ranks and lines established at the marshalling gradually became more and more loose, and after a longish battle there might often arise a situation like the one Polydamas, N 737-9, reports to Hector in relation to the Trojans who had actually been victorious:

οἱ μὲν ἀφεστᾶσιν σὺν τεύχεσιν, οἱ δὲ μάχονται
παυρότεροι πλεόνεσσι, κεδασθέντες κατὰ νῆας.

'Some are now standing idle under arms, while others are scattered among the ships and fighting against greater numbers.' Therefore leaders had constantly to spur on and regroup their men, even in the middle of the battle. But a tightly concentrated formation and firmly established order were particularly necessary in the second type of fighting which we find in the battles of the epic – the massed attack, to an examination of which we now turn.

Massed Attack and the Defence to it

The epic does not, of course, give any tactical rules about this method of fighting either; but the presentation of the described battle scenes is of such a kind that we may infer existing knowledge and practice from it. The prerequisite for achieving the decisive result in battle is, as a rule, the break-through of the enemy lines. This break-through is therefore the purpose and aim of every offensive. I quote a few examples briefly at the beginning, to some of which I shall have to return. Thus it says: Ζ 6 Αἴας ... ῥῆξε φάλαγγας 'Ajax ... broke the line'; Η 141 Ἀρηίθοος ... κορύνῃ ῥήγνυσκε φάλαγγα 'Areithous used an iron mace to smash his way through the enemy ranks'; Ο 615 Ἕκτωρ ... ἔθελεν ῥῆξαι στίχας ἀνδρῶν 'Hector's aim was to break the enemy line'; 617 οὐδ᾽ ὣς δύνατο ῥῆξαι 'but even so he failed to break through'; Λ 537 ἵετο δῦναι ὅμιλον ... ῥῆξαί τε 'he was eager to get in among the throng ... and break through'; Λ 90 σφῇ ἀρετῇ Δαναοὶ ῥήξαντο φάλαγγας 'the Greeks summoned up their courage and broke the enemy lines'; Ν 680 Ἕκτωρ ... ῥηξάμενος Δαναῶν πυκινὰς στίχας ἀσπιστάων 'Hector ... breaking the close ranks of the shield-bearing Greeks'; Ν 718 Λοκροὶ βάλλοντες Τρώων ῥήγνυντο φάλαγγας 'the Locrians by shooting broke through the Trojan ranks'; Ο 409 Τρῶες Δαναῶν ... φάλαγγας ῥηξάμενοι 'the Trojans breaking the Greek lines'; Ρ 285 Αἴας ... Τρώων ἐκέδασσε φάλαγγας, οἳ περὶ Πατρόκλῳ βέβασαν 'Ajax scattered the ranks of the Trojans, who had gathered round Patroclus'; Ο 328, Π 306 ἀνὴρ ἕλεν ἄνδρα κεδασθείσης ὑσμίνης 'Having broken through the ranks, they began to pick off the enemy one by one' (contrast Ο 303, ὑσμίνην ἤρτυνον 'they formed a strong battle-line'), on this schol. BLV[14] τῆς τάξεως διαλυθείσης 'the line having been shattered', Eustat. 1061, 30 διαλυθείσης τῆς κατὰ πύργον ἢ τοῖχον παραβολικῆς ἁρμονίας 'its cohesion, compared in similes to that of a tower or wall, having been shattered'. This is why Achilles, the most outstanding of all Greek heroes, is called ῥηξήνωρ 'breaker of men' Η 228, Ν 324, Π 146, 575, δ 5 which is explained by Apollonius 138, 24: ἀπὸ τοῦ διαρρήσσειν τὰς φάλαγγας, τουτέστι τὰς τάξεις τῶν ἀνδρῶν 'because he broke through the ranks, that is, the lines of men'; and the ῥηξηνορίη, ξ 217, 'the daring that breaks the battle-line' is appropriately explained schol. HPQ: ἀνδρεία παρὰ τὸ ῥηγνύειν τὴν δύναμιν τῶν ἐναντίων 'courage, in breaking the strength of the enemy'. But this ῥηγνύναι 'breaking through' presupposes an offensive, for the defence against which, and for the most part to cause which, it is necessary to use massed troops, which were less in demand in the σταδίη μάχη 'standing fight'.

One particularly brave hero or several together may well succeed in achieving a break-through or a decisive incursion into the lines of already discouraged opponents, **[I.35]** and one does not need to think in terms of poetic embellishment when the poet attributes such a success to a hero as powerful as Hector or Achilles. Rüstow, *Heerwesen* p. 50, discussing the fighting method of Roman legions, reminds us very aptly of the example of Winkelried, whose heroic courage at Sempach made the necessary breach to gain space for the attack with the halberd into the armoured lines of the Austrian knights.[15] So Hector, Ν 151ff., when he unexpectedly comes up against the tightly massed formation of the Greeks, shouts: Τρῶες ... παρμένετ'· οὗτοι δηρὸν ἐμὲ σχήσουσιν Ἀχαιοί, καὶ μάλα πυργηδὸν σφέας αὐτοὺς ἀρτύναντες 'Stand by me, Trojans ... the Greeks will not hold me up for long, packed together though they are like stones in a tower', and later, when he advances at the head of the tightly massed Trojans against the Achaeans, he tests their resistance 807 προποδίζων, εἴ πώς οἱ εἴξειαν ὑπασπίδια προβιβάντι 'going step by step, to see if they would break before him as he moved forward under the cover of his shield', simply from fear of his heroic strength. All the same he does not dare to come really close, so that Ajax shouts at him from the line, 810: σχεδὸν ἐλθέ· τίη δειδίσσεαι αὔτως Ἀργείους 'Come closer. Why are you vainly trying to terrify the Greeks?', cf. also Ο 615ff., Ζ 6. So Achilles also boasts as he calls on the Greeks, Υ 354, μηκέτι νῦν Τρώων ἑκὰς ἔστατε κ. τ. λ. 'don't stand there waiting for the Trojans' etc., 362 ἀλλὰ μάλα στιχὸς εἶμι διαμπερές 'I am going straight through their line', and then, true to his word, leaps among the Trojans, dealing destruction all round him, 381, like a death-defying cavalryman galloping into the enemy square. But these are only special cases.

When a general attack is to be carried out, or an attempt at a break-through by the enemy to be repulsed, the closing together of the lines is a necessary preliminary, and it is the absolute duty of the leader to bring this about. Whether the clash then really ensues is not always

Part I

in the leader's control and depends on other circumstances, but the solidly massed formation must in all cases precede any seriously planned attempt at forcing a decision.

Naturally, all the necessary conditions for this are most favourably met on both sides when the men are first drawn up, because it can then be effected with the least difficulty. It therefore appears absolutely understandable that when two armies which have been drawn up so close together, as was the situation before Pandarus' shot on the first day of fighting, join battle, Δ 281, a collision of the massed troops occurs, a violent clash, which is executed by both sides along the whole line, even if not simultaneously and with the same ferocity. The poet does indeed make such a clash occur, and I do not know how this could be described more poetically and graphically than in verses Δ 446-56:

οἱ δ᾽ ὅτε δή ῥ᾽ ἐς χῶρον ἕνα ξυνιόντες ἵκοντο,
σύν ῥ᾽ ἔβαλον ῥινούς, σὺν δ᾽ ἔγχεα καὶ μένε᾽ ἀνδρῶν
χαλκεοθωρήκων· ἀτὰρ ἀσπίδες ὀμφαλόεσσαι
ἔπληντ᾽ ἀλλήλῃσι, πολὺς δ᾽ ὀρυμαγδὸς ὀρώρει.
ἔνθα δ᾽ ἅμ᾽ οἰμωγή τε καὶ εὐχωλὴ πέλεν ἀνδρῶν
ὀλλύντων τε καὶ ὀλλυμένων, ῥέε δ᾽ αἵματι γαῖα.
ὡς δ᾽ ὅτε χείμαρροι ποταμοὶ κατ᾽ ὄρεσφι ῥέοντες
ἐς μισγάγκειαν συμβάλλετον ὄβριμον ὕδωρ
κρουνῶν ἐκ μεγάλων κοίλης ἔντοσθε χαράδρης ...
ὣς τῶν μισγομένων γένετο ἰαχή τε πόνος τε.

'The armies advanced and met in a single space with a great clash of shields, spears and bronze-armoured warriors. The bossed shields collided and a great roar went up – the screams of the dying, the jeers of the victors – and the earth ran with blood. As two mountain rivers in winter, fed by their great springs higher up, meet in full spate in some deep ravine ... such were the *yelling* and *turmoil* as the two armies *came to grips.*'

The poet does not give us the details of the battle. It can naturally have consisted only of a series of individual fights along the whole line, which can also develop into a group fight around the corpse of a fallen leader or a valuable piece of booty, as we find described for instance in the verses following immediately, Δ 457-72: Antilochus, presumably during the advance, hurls his spear and from very close by hits **[I.36]** Echepolus so that the spear penetrates deep into his head through the ridge of his helmet, and the warrior falls like a tower in the tumult, 462. Elephenor bends down, crouching under his shield (he did not need to leap forward out of the line), to drag the dead man ὑπὲκ βελέων 'from under the missiles', and strip him of his armour; but Agenor, who notices his intention, thrusts his spear into his side where it is visible next to the shield, and so hits him from very close by,

> ... ἐπ᾽ αὐτῷ δ᾽ ἔργον ἐτύχθη
> ἀργαλέον Τρώων καὶ Ἀχαιῶν· οἱ δὲ λύκοι ὣς
> ἀλλήλοις ἐπόρουσαν, ἀνὴρ δ᾽ ἄνδρ᾽ ἐδνοπάλιζεν.

'A grim struggle between Trojans and Greeks developed over him. They leapt at each other like wolves, and man grappled with man.' The general fighting continues until a success has been achieved on one or the other side, or until weariness on both sides leads to the σταδίη μάχη 'standing fight', which the subsequent verses, 473ff., describe to us in a different part of the battle field.

The solidly massed formation which was described above as a necessary preliminary to the clash of arms was only briefly indicated in this passage, Δ 281-2; we find it described in more detail in Π 211, where the situation is similar inasmuch as there also the men go into battle immediately after being drawn up. Achilles himself has drawn up his Myrmidons, who are to go into battle with Patroclus, and as he had done in the past he directs encouraging words to the troops, 200ff. The Myrmidons, hearing the words of their king, close their ranks more tightly, 211ff., as tightly as one fits together from close-set stones a wall to keep out the elements,

> ἀσπὶς ἄρ᾽ ἀσπίδ᾽ ἔρειδε, κόρυς κόρυν, ἀνέρα δ᾽ ἀνήρ·
> ψαῦον δ᾽ ἱππόκομοι κόρυθες λαμπροῖσι φάλοισι
> νευόντων· ὣς πυκνοὶ ἐφέστασαν ἀλλήλοισιν.

'They stood so close together, shield to shield, helmet to helmet, man to man, that when they bent down, the glittering crests of their plumed helmets met.' In these words an exemplary drawing up must be being described to us, effected by the best leader in the Greek army with the most competent men, and the picture of a contingent, tightly massed to right and left, from front to rear, could not be more clearly given. Immediately after this drawing up, the Myrmidons advance with a loud battle cry, 267, against the Trojans fighting closest to them and, like an irritated swarm of wasps, 259, hurl themselves at them in massed formation, 276, ἐν δ᾽ ἔπεσον Τρώεσσιν ἀολλέες 'they fell on the Trojans in a mass'. They, however, do not sustain the attack. Their formations falter, 280, they turn to flight at the first threatened position, and Patroclus hurls his spear into the middle of the thickest throng of retreating men, 285.

If we can regard this drawing up of the Myrmidons as the example of a column of attack, then in the formation described in N 125ff., ordered (as the poet describes it) by no less a person than the god Poseidon himself to halt the Trojans' victorious charge, we have presented to us the model of a defensive formation. Of course, what matters mainly here, as in the other passage, is the tight, firm closing of the ranks, and the avoidance of any gaps by the linking of the shields. N 131-3 therefore read exactly the same as the verses cited above, from ἀσπὶς ἄρ' ἀσπίδ' ἔρειδε to ἀλλήλοισιν. Nevertheless I must stay with this passage for a little longer in order to discuss briefly the following verses. These complete the description but, in my opinion, have not yet been correctly explained, at least in the editions known to me.

I agree with Faesi-Franke's explanation of verse 130 (which is not found in the description of the drawing up of the Myrmidons) φράξαντες δόρυ δουρί, σάκος σάκεϊ προθελύμνῳ: **[I.37]** 'they pushed spear to spear and shield to shield into a fence' so tightly 'that the lowest layer of each (shield) was pushed forward in front of his neighbour's', an arrangement which would automatically result if the warriors closed together from right and left. They also stood so closely behind each other that, when they bent down, the crests of their helmets touched the men in front of them, 132. Then it is further said 134-5:

ἔγχεα δ' ἐπτύσσοντο θρασειάων ἀπὸ χειρῶν
σειόμεν'. οἱ δ' ἰθὺς φρόνεον, μέμασαν δὲ μάχεσθαι.

'and the spears *overlapped* as they brandished them in their sturdy hands. Their minds were fixed on facing the enemy and they were eager for the clash.' The expression ἐπτύσσοντο 'overlapped', which seems to me very important for the poet's correct view of the situation, is the one in whose explanation I particularly differ. In schol. BL it is said of it: κραδαινόμενα πτυσσομένοις ἔοικε 'spears being shaken look as if they are being folded', and in the paraphrase, εἰς τὸ αὐτὸ συνήγετο καὶ ἐκάμπτετο 'they were being brought together, i.e. bent'.[16] Faesi explains, in accordance with this view: 'the spears were brandished by the warlike and excited warriors (θρασειάων ἀπὸ χειρῶν 'in their sturdy hands') with such force that they seemed to bend'. Ameis also explains: 'they bent', as does Düntzer who adds: 'they seemed to bend with the mighty swinging of the hands'; and Passow in the *Lexicon* translates, citing our passage, 'the spears bent'.

But two weighty considerations argue against this explanation of the word ἐπτύσσοντο, one factual and one linguistic. (1) How was it possible, if the warriors were standing in a massed formation man next to man, in front and behind each other, forming a fence with the spear shafts, to brandish their spears, and indeed so violently that they seemed to bend? The men could hardly move their arms, let alone lift them up to brandish a spear. One should just imagine oneself in this position. It is clear that the warriors could well find space for a thrust, but they could not lift their arms over their heads and brandish their spears.

Giseke in the *Lexicon Homericum* therefore dissociates himself, rightly, from this view, but, as I think, has still not found the correct one, corresponding to the meaning of the word as well as to the situation, when he explains: 'the spears as they moved formed a regular layer; they were all on the same level, like a fold'.

For (2) what does πτύσσω mean? Can the word anyway have the meaning 'to bend', which is attributed to it above? The basic meaning is: to fold, to heap together several times, to stack, to place on top of each other in layers, e.g. εἵματα 'clothes', χιτῶνα 'a tunic'; πτύχες are the *strata* or layers of the shields.[17] The word retains this basic meaning in our passage too. ἔγχεα ἐπτύσσοντο means: 'the spears were set over each other in layers.' This is the natural consequence of the drawing up. Since we are dealing with a tightly massed column which is at least two lines deep and about to face an enemy attack, the first line present their spears and lower them, – just as is described in P 355, σάκεσσι ... ἔρχατο ... πρὸ δὲ δούρατ' ἔχοντο 'with a fence of shields and levelled spears' – so that, if they are properly lined up, as they should be in an exemplary drawing up, they form one layer. The second line must push through with its spears between the shoulders of the men in front, and thus creates the second layer – which is necessary for the notion of πτύσσειν. So the spears do not lie on the same level but on at least two, and thus strictly speaking form two layers. I do not venture any opinion on whether a third line also thrust through with their spears; but we must assume at least two lines standing one behind the other with their spears lowered, according to the words of the epic. Now I understand the participle σειόμενα, 135, 'being shaken' to mean that as long as the warriors were still moving into position to produce the massed formation, the spears had of course to be held high, for otherwise a closing of the ranks **[I.38]** could not be achieved, and that the lowering and thrusting through occurred (i.e. the spears were lowered or generally set in motion and arranged in layers above each other) only when the men in front and the ones behind had taken their correct places. I find confirmation for the idea that the poet of our passage imagines the spears ready for a thrust, not for a throw, in verse 147: οἱ δ' ἀντίοι υἷες Ἀχαιῶν *νύσσοντες* ξίφεσίν τε καὶ ἔγχεσιν ἀμφιγύοισιν ὦσαν ἀπὸ σφείων, sc. Ἕκτορα, 'and the Greeks facing Hector *lunged* at him with swords and spears with leaf-shaped tips and forced him to retreat', in which the word ξίφεσιν 'swords' may indicate that men were standing in the formation who had either already thrown their spears, or were armed only with the sword (perhaps together with a bow), an inequality of equipment which we have met before. It is interesting that Polybius (XVIII 29. 6), in describing the Macedonian phalanx, quotes N 131-4, saying ὡς Ὅμηρος ὑποδείκνυσιν ἐν τούτοις 'as Homer indicates in these lines', to illustrate the πύκνωσις κατ' ἐπιστάτην καὶ κατὰ παραστάτην 'its close order in relation to depth and breadth'.

At all events, in this massed defensive formation the Greeks feel safe and ready for battle again after their previous loss of morale, even ready for an offensive: 135 ἰθὺς φρόνεον, μέμασαν δὲ μάχεσθαι 'Their minds were fixed on facing the enemy and they were eager for the clash.' But the Trojans under Hector's leadership, and this also is typical, do not dare to attack the massed formation, in spite of Hector's confident words 150ff. They rather advance one by one, cautiously and protected by their shields, 158, to provoke the Greeks to battle; and out of this a σταδίη μάχη 'standing fight' develops, 159-332.

A real clash of massed troops which ensued is described to us immediately afterwards. N 337-44, τῶν ὁμόσ' ἦλθε μάχη, μέμασαν δ' ... ἀλλήλους καθ' ὅμιλον ἐναιρέμεν ... ἔφριξεν δὲ μάχη ... ἐγχείησιν ... ὄσσε δ' ἄμερδεν αὐγὴ χαλκείη κορύθων ... θωρήκων ... σακέων ... ἐρχομένων ἄμυδις 'so the front lines massed ... and ... every man longed to kill his opponent. The battlefield bristled with spears ... and the eye was dazzled by the glint of bronze from the helmets ... breastplates ... and shields as the two armies came together.' It goes without saying that during a general attack the battle cry is raised, but usually it is expressly mentioned; I only quote the passage which clearly refers to it, Ξ 148: Poseidon shouts like nine thousand or ten thousand men ἐν πολέμῳ, ἔριδα ξυνάγοντες Ἄρηος 'in war, when they join the strife of battle'.

The picture of the closing together of the Greeks in the face of Hector's attempts at a break-through, O 615ff., is very vivid. Hector wanted ῥῆξαι στίχας ἀνδρῶν 'to break the enemy line' and indeed he tried to do this, as the bravest of heroes, ᾗ δὴ πλεῖστον ὅμιλον ὅρα καὶ τεύχε' ἄριστα 'where he saw the greatest numbers and best-armed men'. But he did not succeed, for the Achaeans

> ἴσχον ... πυργηδὸν ἀρηρότες, ἠΰτε πέτρη
> ἠλίβατος μεγάλη, πολιῆς ἁλὸς ἐγγὺς ἐοῦσα,
> ἥτε μένει λιγέων ἀνέμων λαιψηρὰ κέλευθα
> κύματά τε τροφόεντα, τά τε προσερεύγεται αὐτήν.

'Packed as tight as the stones in a wall, they held firm like a great sheer cliff that faces the grey sea and resists the onslaught of the howling winds and vast waves roaring in at it.' Fresh attacks are repeatedly made, 624, until finally, just as a herd scatters when a lion leaps into its midst, 635, 637, the Achaeans are all put to flight by Hector and Father Zeus; image emerging as reality, perhaps, because he had successfully broken into their lines, like the lion who leapt into the herd. The explanation by Faesi and Ameis, that the general flight here was caused by the killing of one single Achaean, 638, πάντες (sc. ἐφοβήθησαν), ὁ δ᾽ οἶον ἔπεφνε Μυκηναῖον Περιφήτην 'The whole Greek force was put to flight, but Hector killed just one Greek, the Mycenaean Periphetes' cannot be correct, since Periphetes falls only when he has already turned round to flee and so has his shield slung round his back, 645. This shield accounts for his fall, and after that Hector thrusts his spear into his chest, 647, 649. It is typical of the Achaeans' fear that none of his friends, although they are still very near him, dares to bring help to him in his need, 651. So I translate ἔπεφνε in verse 638 above as 'he killed', not as 'he had killed'.

[I.39] In Π 562ff. another general advance is described to us. After previous encouragement of the men by their leaders, strong columns are formed on both sides, 563, ἀμφοτέρωθεν ἐκαρτύναντο φάλαγγας 'the two forces had strengthened their ranks', during which, of course, all the warriors who have leapt forward must have stepped back into the line; then they run together with a loud battle cry, so that their armour rings out, 566, and Zeus spreads darkness over the κρατερὴ ὑσμίνη 'the field of battle', to make the struggle of the fighting over Sarpedon's corpse all the more terrible, 568. With their first assault the Trojans throw back the Achaeans, 569; at this Patroclus leaps forward, hurls a mighty stone and scares the lines of the Trojans into retreating some distance, 588; for a time there is a 'standing fight', and from 633 a general push forward again, initiated by Meriones, is described:

ὣς τῶν ὤρνυτο δοῦπος ἀπὸ χθονὸς εὐρυοδείης
χαλκοῦ τε ῥινοῦ τε βοῶν τ᾽ εὐποιητάων
νυσσομένων ξίφεσίν τε καὶ ἔγχεσιν ἀμφιγύοισιν.

'So from the broad earth there rose the thud of bronze, leather and well-made shields as men *lunged* at each other with swords and spears.'

The difference between a massed battle and a 'standing fight' is clearly emphasised in the superb description of the bloody struggle which has developed over Protesilaus' ship, O 707ff.

δήουν ἀλλήλους αὐτοσχεδόν· οὐδ᾽ ἄρα τοί γε
τόξων ἀϊκὰς ἀμφὶς μένον οὐδέ τ᾽ ἀκόντων

'They hacked at each other hand-to-hand. It was not a matter now of

70

keeping their distance and weathering volleys of arrows or spears on either side' (as happened in the σταδίη μάχη 'standing fight', where one watched for the arrows and spears whistling in from further apart), but, 'standing man to man', ἐγγύθεν ἱστάμενοι, they fought in their fury with all the weapons that came to their hands, with axes and hatchets, with swords and spears, ῥέε δ' αἵματι γαῖα μέλαινα, 715 'the earth ran black with blood'.

But the difference becomes particularly evident when the two types of fighting are contrasted with each other in the epic, as happens in the battles for Patroclus' corpse. After advances have been made by both sides with varying fortune, in the same way as in the battle for the fallen Sarpedon, – P 262 Τρῶες προὔτυψαν ἀολλέες 'the Trojans pressed forward in a mass'; 266 αὐτὰρ Ἀχαιοὶ ἔστασαν ... φραχθέντες σάκεσιν χαλκήρεσιν 'the Greeks faced them, making a fence of their bronze shields'; 274 ὦσαν δὲ πρότεροι Τρῶες ... Ἀχαιούς 'at first the Trojans pushed back the ... Greeks'; then, after Ajax has brought the latter to stand their ground again, 278, Αἴας ῥεῖα ... Τρώων ἐκέδασσε φάλαγγας, οἳ περὶ Πατρόκλῳ βέβασαν 285 'Ajax easily scattered the ranks of Trojans, who had gathered round Patroclus' – we are told that the Trojans, because they were poor spirited, would have gone all the way back to Ilium if Apollo had not especially exhorted Aeneas and urged him on to new deeds, 322ff.; then the latter, with encouraging words and his own brave example, 342 πολὺ προμάχων ἐξάλμενος ἔστη 'he leapt forward to make a stand well in front of the foremost fighters', makes the Trojans rally and leads them in a new attack against the Danaans. But Ajax immediately orders his men into a defensive formation, 354ff. σάκεσσι γὰρ ἔρχατο πάντῃ ἑσταότες περὶ Πατρόκλῳ, πρὸ δὲ δούρατ' ἔχοντο 'They had surrounded Patroclus with a fence of shields and levelled spears'. Then he himself walks along the lines inspecting them, μάλα πάντας ἐπῴχετο 'he went round them all' and gives strict orders that no one should withdraw from the corpse or even think of leaping forward into battle from out of the line; they are all to remain standing in massed formation and only σχεδόθεν μάχεσθαι, 359 'fight hand-to-hand'. So a bloody struggle ensued, during which the fighting men ἀγχιστῖνοι ἔπιπτον, 361 'fell in heaps'. But the Trojan losses were still greater than those of the Achaeans, because in this battle between closed ranks the latter understood better how to cover and protect each other, 364 μέμνηντο γὰρ αἰεὶ ἀλλήλους καθ' ὅμιλον ἀλεξέμεναι φόνον αἰπύν 'they remembered all the time in the mêlée to protect each other from death'. In contrast to this terrible, dangerous and arduous battle, however, we are told in the following verses, 370ff., of a far more relaxed 'standing **[I.40]** fight', which moreover took place in bright sunlight whereas those others fought in mist. There it says: οἱ δ' ἄλλοι Τρῶες καὶ ἐυκνήμιδες Ἀχαιοὶ εὔκηλοι πόλεμιζον ὑπ' αἰθέρι ... μεταπαυόμενοι δ' ἐμάχοντο 'The other Trojans and Greek men-at-arms were *battling at their ease* under a clear sky ... They had *periods of rest* during the fight'; and this is characteristic of the σταδίη μάχη 'standing fight', as the following, 374, is too, ἀλλήλων ἀλεείνοντες βέλεα στονόεντα, πολλὸν ἀφεσταότες, τοὶ δ' ἐν μέσῳ ἄλγε' ἔπασχον ἠέρι καὶ πολέμῳ κ. τ. λ. 'they *kept their distance* and *avoided each others' spears*. It was only in the centre that they were suffering badly from the mist and *the battle*' and so on.

Before I turn to the next section I must briefly mention one more point concerning the attack in a massed line, viz. the holding of the spears. In the defensive formation established by Poseidon, Ν 130ff. (discussed above), the spears had been lowered in expectation of the enemy, ἐπτύσσοντο 'they overlapped', νύσσοντες 'lunging', cf. Ρ 355, πρὸ δὲ δούρατ' ἔχοντο 'a fence of levelled spears'. But in Ρ 233 during the Trojan attack induced by Hector's promises and encouragement it is said: οἱ δ' ἰθὺς Δαναῶν βρίσαντες ἔβησαν δούρατ' ἀνασχόμενοι '*they lifted their spears and charged* at the Greeks with full force'. The expression ἀνέχεσθαι 'lift' recurs several times in relation to the spear lifted above the head for a throw (Ⴑ 655, Φ 67, 161, τ 448 in relation to individual heroes and Λ 594 and Ο 298 for a column). In Λ 593 the Achaeans mass around Eurypylus to receive the hard-pressed, retreating Ajax, σάκε' ὤμοισι κλίναντες, δούρατ' ἀνασχόμενοι, 'behind sloped shields, with their spears up at the ready' and in Ο 298 (the passage which has already been mentioned once[18] and is more important for our examination), Thoas calls on the best of the Achaeans to hold their position against the advancing Trojans: στείομεν, εἴ κεν πρῶτον ἐρύξομεν ἀντιάσαντες δούρατ' ἀνασχόμενοι 'let us make a stand, with our spears up at the ready, in the hope of holding the attack.' It then says that the Achaeans, in response to his call, ὑσμίνην ἤρτυνον ... Τρώεσσιν ἐναντίον 'formed a battle-line ... against the Trojans'. Then, under Hector's leadership, the Trojans advance in a massed formation and with a loud battle cry a volley of weapons is thrown from both sides, 313. In their weakened state the Achaeans were not in a position to sustain a real Trojan attack; all that mattered to them was to gain time while the main army retreated, and to delay the victorious advancing enemy for a time, 297. They were therefore standing there holding their spears above their heads ready for throwing – one could almost translate 'ready to shoot' – and achieved their purpose completely: the Trojans, faced with the threat of immediate retaliation, did not advance to attack but first halted and tried to throw the Greek lines into confusion with a volley of spear throws. We must explain in the same way the expression in the passage mentioned first, Ρ 233: the Trojans went forward to attack the Danaans, with firm steps, spears ready for the throw, not to throw individually and one after the other, as in a 'standing fight', but to launch a salvo. Faced with this, the Danaans retreated even before the Trojans had come within shooting range, P 275 ὑπέτρεσαν, οὐδέ τιν' αὐτῶν Τρῶες ὑπέρθυμοι ἕλον ἔγχεσιν, ἱέμενοί περ 'they gave ground, and the proud Trojans did not succeed in killing any of them with their spears, for all their efforts'.

For the advance to attack with lowered spears, we find a description in the case of the battle-hardened, brave Abantes B 543ff. that they are said to be αἰχμηταί, μεμαῶτες ὀρεκτῆσιν μελίῃσι θώρηκας ῥήξειν δηΐων ἀμφὶ στήθεσσιν 'fighters aiming to lunge with their ash spears and rip through the armour on their enemies' chests'. So, depending on circumstances, a more or less closed mass could attack as well as defend with spears lifted high for throwing or lowered for thrusting.

Although many other examples could be cited which perhaps would make the case even stronger, I must break off here to devote a brief discussion to flight and pursuit, which conclude the picture of a battle.

[1.41] Retreat, Flight and Pursuit

The purpose of attack and fighting in the open field is to force the enemy to flight. This is achieved when the enemy line is broken. However, the losing side, before it flees, sometimes has open to it the far less dangerous option of retreat, and on this subject we find in the descriptions of the epic clear evidence of a certain tactical understanding. We even have to distinguish between a simple retreat carried out by the whole army while still fighting, and an organised rearguard action, carried out by a smaller section of the army to protect the retreating majority.

The poet gives us the picture of a slow retreat during battle in Ε 590ff. At Ares' command, the fleeing Trojans have again been brought to a halt. Spurred on by Sarpedon, Hector has left his chariot and drawn up his men afresh, 495, and advances once more against the Achaeans, who stand up to him. First, a 'standing fight' develops which brings losses to both sides, 533-90, until Hector leads his formations in an assault with the help of the War God himself and Enyo striding in front, 592. Alarmed at the sight of them, Diomedes orders retreat, but a fighting retreat, 605: ἀλλὰ πρὸς Τρῶας τετραμμένοι αἰὲν ὀπίσσω εἴκετε, μηδὲ θεοῖς μενεαινέμεν ἶφι μάχεσθαι 'Retreat then, but facing the enemy. Do not try to offer battle to the gods.'

The poet seems to indicate that the retreat is taken more seriously by some of the Greeks, since at 608 he has Hector kill two Greeks on one chariot which they must have just mounted in order to withdraw from the battle; elsewhere chariots are not mounted during the slow retreat, and all the heroes appear on foot. In the description, however, we are made clearly aware that, in accordance with Diomedes' order, we are dealing with a fighting retreat. This is shown by the fact that individual heroes still leap forward from the Greek lines to fight with Trojans who have done likewise, like individual marksmen in a retreating line who stop to fire another shot at the pursuing enemy: thus Ajax, 610, who is even able to regain his spear but then at once retreats, 622; Tlepolemus 628ff.; indeed, Odysseus for a time even gains a considerable success against the Lycians, 677, but without thereby bringing about a change in the course of the battle. For that the Greeks are continuing in a fighting retreat is expressly stated in 699ff.:

Ἀργεῖοι δ' ὑπ' Ἄρηϊ καὶ Ἕκτορι χαλκοκορυστῇ
οὔτε ποτὲ προτρέποντο μελαινάων ἐπὶ νηῶν
οὔτε ποτ' ἀντεφέροντο μάχῃ, ἀλλ' αἰὲν ὀπίσσω
χάζονθ', ὡς ἐπύθοντο μετὰ Τρώεσσιν Ἄρηα.

'But the Greeks, faced by the War-god Ares and Hector in his bronze armour, neither turned towards their black ships nor counter-attacked, but *fell back steadily* when they became aware of Ares' presence on the Trojan side.'

Because so many Achaeans were falling at Hector's hands, 703ff., the retreat would probably have turned into a real rout if Athene and Hera had not decided on their part to go on the offensive (718: ἀλλ' ἄγε δὴ καὶ νῶϊ μεδώμεθα θούριδος ἀλκῆς 'Come: time for the two of us to call up that fighting spirit of ours!') and to give support to the Achaeans who were bravely defending themselves under Diomedes, 781ff. As a result, after the removal of Ares the situation is reversed, ending in the flight of the Trojans after Ajax has broken through their lines, Z 6ff.

The picture of an organised rearguard action, on the other hand, is clearly presented to us in the passage discussed above, O 281ff. After Hector was knocked out, the Greeks had pursued close at the heels of the wildly fleeing Trojans, 277ff. But because of the utterly **[I.42]** unexpected re-appearance of Hector whom Apollo had healed and filled with new courage and confidence of victory, they are greatly alarmed and utterly disheartened, 279-80. It is now necessary to beat a retreat and, at this sudden turn of events, to bring back to the safety of the ships, with as little damage as possible, the mass of the Greek army, which has lost cohesion in the hasty pursuit and is therefore no longer in a state to fight effectively. In this difficult situation, the advice to this effect is put in the mouth of Thoas, who was, 281ff.:

Part I

Αἰτωλῶν ὄχ' ἄριστος, ἐπιστάμενος μὲν ἄκοντι,
ἐσθλὸς δ' ἐν σταδίῃ· ἀγορῇ δέ ἑ παῦροι Ἀχαιῶν
νίκων, ὁππότε κοῦροι ἐρίσσειαν περὶ μύθων,

'by far the best of the Aetolians, skilled with the spear and a good man in the standing fight; and there were few Greeks who surpassed him in the assembly when they competed to give the best advice', and whose high esteem is probably best indicated by the fact that Poseidon, N 216, chose his appearance in order to spur on the despondent Achaeans, since θεὸς ὣς τίετο δήμῳ 'he was honoured like a god by the people'. So this man advises, 295ff., that the bulk of the army should withdraw to the ships, but that the best heroes should stay in position, spears over their heads ready to throw, to try and see whether they can hold up the victorious Trojans for a time. His advice is followed, and Ajax, Idomeneus, Teucer, Meriones and Meges with their men – for this is how I understand οἱ μὲν ἄρ' ἀμφ' Αἴαντα κ. τ. λ. 'those under the leadership of Ajax' etc. – establish a well ordered battle line against Hector and the Trojans, ὑσμίνην ἤρτυνον, 303 'they formed a battle-line', while the main bulk of the army retreats to the ships, 305.

Even if some of the misgivings expressed about this passage, Thoas' advice, (cf. Hentze, *Appendix* to O, p. 103), may appear justified, and its original connection with the description as a whole may appear debatable, this is of minor importance for our investigation. Its author has in any case given us a clear picture of an intelligently organised rearguard action. It goes without saying that such an undertaking cannot be achieved by five individual heroes, 301-2, against a victorious enemy; the heroes named do it with their men. One unit of the army covers the retreat while the bulk seeks safety at the ships, and, facing this rearguard action, the Trojans on their side have also reestablished in their ranks the order which had been destroyed. If this is right, some of the difficulties compiled by Hentze, loc. cit., seem to me to lose their force. It is quite possible to reconcile with Thoas' advice the προὔτυψαν ἀολλέες, 306 '(The Trojans) advanced in a mass' and the ὑπέμειναν ἀολλέες, 312 '(The Greeks) awaited them in mass formation'; so too the flying arrows mentioned in 313 and discussed above, and the comparison with a herd, 323. These points, which have been emphasised as misgivings about the passage, prove exactly that its composer very sensibly has the cover executed by a whole detachment, not by a few heroes, and that we are justified in talking about a genuine rearguard action. I therefore cannot accept another reservation made by Ameis about 295, 'that the ensuing narrative does not assume that Thoas' advice was followed'. On the contrary, everything seems to me to proceed in order. In 306 the Trojans advance in a closed mass, and volleys are fired from both sides; then the Trojans, under Apollo's leadership, push forward with a loud battle cry, 320-1, and the Achaeans cannot hold their position (their numbers were of course inferior); the battle line is shattered, and the valiant band which had covered the retreat and delayed the enemy for a time follows the majority back to the ships in complete flight, 326ff.

We now move on to a discussion of actual flight. It is a natural consequence of the method of fighting portrayed and the type of weapons used that flight is the most dangerous and bloodiest act of the battle for the weaker side. From the moment a part of the army turns its back, it effectively hands over every weapon **[I.43]** to its opponents, who now, without any great danger to themselves, can create havoc among the fleeing enemy for as long as their stamina holds out. Speed alone is decisive in finding safety and pursuing success, and therefore the best means of achieving this, the chariot, is immediately used on both sides.

In consequence there are two typical features of the descriptions of flight and pursuit as we find them in rich abundance in the epic, and we should regard them as drawn from real life: first, on both sides, for flight and pursuit, chariots are mounted; second – something which stands out even more – only warriors on the fleeing side are killed. I have already mentioned above that in the moment that the army turns to flight, it must have been especially difficult to mount the chariot quickly, and that, then above all, special demands were made on the loyalty and trustworthiness of the charioteer. The poet takes this situation into account in that, at the beginning of a rout, he repeatedly has heroes on the defeated side fall at the very moment when they are mounting their chariot or have just done so.

Now whereas during a retreat (see above), order was on the whole maintained, during a rout the cohesion of the lines, which was loose anyway, very soon completely dissolved. The leaders and nobles would try to mount their chariots, drive through the crowds of fleeing infantry and often hurry far ahead of them, thus removing from them their last means of making a stand and resisting. The warrior's arms protected him only inadequately during flight, since if he slung the long shield over his back, he was in danger of tripping at every leap forward, and the small round shield which the great majority carried gave only little protection to the back. An additional fact was that, in this type of battle, especially when flight had been caused by a breakthrough into the lines, the enemy were on the heels of the vanquished immediately, and were able to knock them down or stab them at will, while they were in no position even to turn round quickly.

To bring to a halt a throng of men who were in flight and being pursued like this was of course possible only through an extraordinary intervention, and so in the epic it is almost always the mighty influence of a god which brings about this turn. But it certainly seems to correspond to the real world if in such a case the current victors too find themselves in difficulties, since they are equally disadvantaged by the loosened order. The lines of the pursuers too rapidly lost their cohesion, since everybody thought only of cutting down the nearest opponent and seizing his weapons as plunder before pushing further forward with his comrades. Now if the fleeing enemy turned and made a stand because of some effective assistance, the pursuers too had to regroup and organise themselves at once, and quite often we find that the tables are suddenly turned and the fugitive turns into the pursuer; or the poet makes a particular point of a situation in which those who have been the victors so far hold their position against an attack by opponents who have regrouped. This is the reason why the Dorians avoided pursuit, because their strength consisted in their close order which was, however, gradually lost in hand-to-hand fighting, cf. Jähns, op. cit., p. 54.

It is wholly in accordance with the nature of a warlike people and the image we should build up for ourselves of the heroic courage and strength of its leaders and princes that the brave heroes on the side of the vanquished should attempt to force a reversal of fortune, and through a courageous offensive delay the victorious pursuer and create a chance for their own side to regroup. These attempts are usually carried out on chariots, and are almost never left unmentioned by the poet when he describes a rout. For simplicity's sake I shall discuss these only after a brief examination of the course of events in a flight and pursuit as described in the epic – to which I now turn.

[I.44]Right at the start of the first battle-day, we are presented with a picture of a rout. Athene had removed Ares, who had been aiding the Trojans, from the battle, Ε 35, and the consequence was, 37, Τρῶας δ᾽ ἔκλιναν Δαναοί 'the Greeks pushed back the Trojans'. (The expression ἔκλιναν Τρῶας 'pushed back the Trojans' is very typical of this action; even more specific is ι 59 κλῖναν δαμάσαντες 'they defeated and pushed back' or Ξ 510 ἔκλινε μάχην 'he swayed the battle'. Its original meaning is presumably: they bent the battle line of the Trojans, made it buckle inwards, as they pressed forwards. This clearly indicates the attempt at resistance by the battle line, which (as it were) strains to remain straight, but is bent inwards by the strong pressure and then broken.) Immediately after the κλῖναι 'pushing back' the flight begins, and only the names of Trojan heroes are listed as killed, 38ff. Agamemnon hurls Odius out of the chariot he has just mounted for flight, and Idomeneus kills Phaestus ἵππων ἐπιβησόμενον 46, 'just as he was getting onto his chariot'; τὸν μὲν ἄρ᾽ Ἰδομενῆος ἐσύλευον θεράποντες 48, 'Idomeneus' followers then stripped his body', it says further, while he himself goes in pursuit of the enemy; Menelaus hits Scamandrius πρόσθεν ἕθεν φεύγοντα μετάφρενον 56, 'as he fled before him, in the middle of the back'; Meriones hits Phereclus whom he κατέμαρπτε διώκων 65, 'pursued and caught'; Meges hits Pedaeus ἐγγύθεν ἐλθών 72, 'when he caught this man up'; and Eurypylus hits Hypsenor πρόσθεν ἕθεν φεύγοντα, μεταδρομάδην ... ὦμον φασγάνῳ ἀΐξας 'as he fled before him, at full tilt he (slashed at) his shoulder with his sword'. So the epic gives us a series of precise individual scenes which are taken from the overall picture of a flight. In the real world, we should not of course imagine just six or ten heroes laying into fleeing opponents, but as many as possible throwing their spears into the mass of fugitives or hacking with their swords when the spears have been thrown. Just as little does a brave hero who has killed a fleeing opponent content himself with the slaughter of the one, but he continues on after those in flight, as is expressly stated in the case of Idomeneus, 48. Diomedes distinguished himself more than all; one often saw him in the middle of the fleeing Trojans, so that one could not make out whether he belonged to the Trojan or Achaean side, 85; for him it was therefore not enough αἰὲν ἀποκτείνειν τὸν ὀπίστατον 'always to kill the hindmost', cf. Θ 342, but he leapt into the middle of the crowd of fugitives, creating havoc and slaughter there, 93.

The Greek leaders all appear on foot, but of course their chariots are following them, so that, after he is wounded by Pandarus' arrow, Diomedes can go back and have the arrow pulled out of the wound by his charioteer, 107. Incidentally, it seems to me very characteristic, and fitting the situation, that in the general flight it was an archer of all men who hit the awesome Diomedes; for such a man with his light arms was most likely to venture to turn round and take a shot at the pursuers. After his wound has been rapidly healed, Tydeus' son again storms after the Trojans in the front line, 134, and now rages among the frightened enemy with trebled fury and the blood lust of a lion, as only a Homeric hero is capable of doing, 136ff.; he no longer strips his enemies of their armour and begins to strike them down in pairs. It is typical that here the poet has this bloody fate befall three pairs of brothers at the hands of Diomedes, 144, 148, 160; and thus, to mark the extraordinary menace of Tydeus' son, he expands a set motif in flight descriptions, viz. that two brothers, usually found on a single chariot, cf. 160, are cut down.

Hector, too, had been swept off with them in desperate flight, during which the Trojans were massacred without resistance, 465, and only the intervention of a god could bring about a change. This is initiated by Apollo who sends Ares to help the Trojans and, through him, spurs them to renewed resistance, 461ff. Sarpedon is the first to regain his heroic courage, 471, and, furious at the Trojans' cowardice, gets Hector to halt the flight and begin battle afresh.

I need to dwell a moment longer on the verses which now follow, Ŀ 493ff., because **[I.45]** if one goes into the context more precisely their explanation up to now, in particular of verse 505, seems to me untenable. Hector, responding to Sarpedon's demand, has leapt out of his chariot, 494, and, brandishing his spear, drives the Trojan army into battle anew. At that, the Trojans do an about-turn and go into action against the Achaeans, 497. What is the situation on both sides now? The Greeks had been engaged in heated pursuit, their ranks more or less disordered in the process; those pursuing by chariot are of course at the front; the chariots of heroes who had remained on foot have also been driven along behind their masters. Now, strengthened by divine assistance, the Trojans suddenly turn. Hector, carried along by his swift horses, has hurried ahead of all the Trojans in flight, and naturally first stops those at the front; as the men who arrive later run up one by one and quickly get themselves in order, a kind of formation is soon created which can move against the Greeks. But the Greeks ὑπέμειναν ἀολλέες, οὐδ' ἐφόβηθεν 'held their ground in massed formation and did not retreat', 498. (I expressly draw attention to the aorists in this passage which indicate the beginning of resistance, as opposed to the imperfects, 527, ὡς Δαναοὶ Τρῶας μένον ἔμπεδον οὐδ' ἐφέβοντο 'so the Greeks held firm against the Trojans and refused to panic', which retrospectively emphasise the holding of this position after a detailed description of it). But for the Greeks to be able to stand up to the advancing Trojans in a closed formation, all the chariots which are still at the front after the pursuit must quickly drive back and clear the front line. The leaders, who were previously standing on their chariots, have of course descended and entered the formation.

These preparations, which were necessary for standing up to the approaching Trojans, and the calm awaiting of the danger, are described to us by the poet in lines 499-527. There we read: As the threshing floor turns white from the chaff which has been winnowed, so the Achaeans turn white, λευκοὶ ὕπερθε γένοντο 503, 'were whitened from above' by the dust which the hooves of the horses whirled up through their lines; 505-6, ἵππων ἂψ ἐπιμισγομένων· ὑπὸ δ' ἔστρεφον ἡνιοχῆες· οἱ δὲ μένος χειρῶν ἰθὺς φέρον 'as the chariots came back among them; for the charioteers wheeled them round; they engaged the enemy full on at close quarters.' Now the commentators refer ἐπιμισγομένων 'came among them' to the Trojans, and explain, Faesi: 505 'when they (the horses of the Trojans) again came among them (the Achaeans), again penetrated into their lines', 506 'οἱ δέ "they" namely Τρῶες "the Trojans", the ἐπιβάται "chariot fighters" as opposed to the ἵππων "chariots" '; in the same way Ameis, La Roche, Düntzer.

But it seems to me that this explanation creates an utterly impossible situation. For, apart from the fact that the understanding of Τρώων 'Trojan' with ἵππων ἐπιμισγομένων 'the chariots came among them' and the reference of οἱ δέ 'they' to the Trojans is very artificial and harsh after lines 502ff., and that cavalry squadrons are nowhere at all described as galloping into foot-soldiers, even if one did assume such a state of affairs – the penetration of hostile chariot fighters into the Greek lines – the result would still not be appropriate; indeed the effect would be almost comic if the poet could only report that this caused the Greeks to be covered in dust. Furthermore, it would be utterly inconceivable that they nevertheless still calmly μένον, 'waited', immobile as a layer of cloud stationary on mountain-tops when there is no breath of wind, 522; that, although the Trojan chariot fighters had penetrated the Greek lines, the son of Atreus ἀν' ὅμιλον ἐφοίτα πολλὰ κελεύων 'went through the ranks, issuing orders', 528; that he then hurled his spear at the Trojans, whose chariot fighters must have already then been fighting behind his back, and hit a πρόμος ἀνήρ 'leading fighter', 533; and that a 'standing battle', as is described in the following verses, would have been able to develop at all.

I therefore leave ἵππων ἐπιμισγομένων 'the chariots came among them' in its natural reference to Ἀχαιοί 'Achaeans', the subject of the sentence, and translate: 'the Achaeans were covered in the dust which the horses whirled up through their lines when they came back and among them again, for the chariot drivers turned them round; but they themselves, namely the chariot fighters, were ready to turn to fighting with their strong arms'. φέρον 'engaged' 506, is used in a 'conative' sense – 'endeavoured to engage' – and ἰθύς 'full on' of the offensive movement **[I.46]** in contrast to the chariots which are driving back. The ἵπποι ἐπιμισγόμενοι 'chariots coming among them' are therefore in my opinion the Greek chariots which had been at the front during the pursuit, and, in the sudden change that occurred, immediately drove back behind the front through the lines of the Greeks that had not yet closed and through other gaps, while their commanders, like the other Achaeans, prepared themselves for battle. Now there only remains the question whether ἐπιμίσγομαι allows this meaning 'to come among them', and this seems to me without doubt to be the case according to linguistic usage. The word primarily describes the mixing of different things which do not strictly speaking belong together. It is used in this general sense in ζ 205: οὐδέ τις ἄμμι βροτῶν ἐπιμίσγεται ἄλλος 'no other mortal comes among us' and 241: Φαιήκεσσ' ὅδ' ἀνὴρ ἐπιμίξεται ἀντιθέοισιν 'this man will come among the god-like Phaeacians'. Apart from our passage it appears once more in the *Iliad*, K 548, where Nestor says to Odysseus and Diomedes, who have returned from their spying mission with the fine horses of Rhesus: 'Where do the magnificent horses come from? I have never seen them before, although I αἰεὶ μὲν Τρώεσσ᾽ ἐπιμίσγομαι, οὐδέ τί φημι μιμνάζειν παρὰ νηυσί, γέρων περ ἐὼν πολεμιστής 'am always encountering the Trojans – for I can claim that I never stay behind by the ships, old as I am for a fighting man'. In this passage the word can very well have the meaning 'I meet in battle'; but Nestor's main purpose is probably to say that he 'comes among the Trojans' more or less in the sense in which he says of himself in Δ 322ff.:

... νῦν αὖτέ με γῆρας ὀπάζει.
ἀλλὰ καὶ ὣς ἱππεῦσι μετέσσομαι ἠδὲ κελεύσω
βουλῇ καὶ μύθοισι· τὸ γὰρ γέρας ἐστὶ γερόντων.
αἰχμὰς δ᾽ αἰχμάσσουσι νεώτεροι, οἵ περ ἐμεῖο
ὁπλότεροι γεγάασι πεποίθασίν τε βίηφιν.

'... now age presses hard upon me. Yet for all that I shall still be with my charioteers and in command. Their plans and orders come from me – that's the privilege of age – even if the spear is left to younger men than myself, who can rely on their muscle.'
So in our passage the word would have more the general meaning 'who came among them again', in conjunction with δι᾽ αὐτῶν, 503, 'drove through their lines'. And since also the adverb ἐπιμίξ 'all together', which occurs five times, is in three passages used especially of the mixing of horses and men, Λ 525, Φ 16, Ψ 242, and in two passages in a more general sense, the explanation given above seems to me quite natural and appropriate to the state of affairs, as well as linguistically unobjectionable.

After many a change and prolonged fluctuation in the battle, it is reported at Z 6 that Ajax has succeeded in breaking through the Trojan formation. It is now all up with them, and the poet immediately follows this with descriptions of scenes characteristic of the beginning of flight. Diomedes kills Axylus together with his chariot driver, 18. Euryalus kills in pairs first Dresus and Opheltius, then the brothers Aisepus and Pedasus whom he strips of their armour. The Trojans flee towards the city in utter confusion, 41; without resistance they are butchered by the Greeks, and only Trojan heroes bleed at the hands of their pursuers, 29-36. Those who have a chariot at their disposal mount it but in their panic pay no attention to where they are going; so Adrestus' horses break their shaft on a tree root, 38, and wildly stampede after the others that are fleeing, while their master is flung out and falls into the hands of his pursuers. Such confusion offers a good opportunity to acquire valuable booty which the traders from Lemnos are happy later to exchange for a drop of good wine, H

473ff., and many a man may well bend down to appropriate valuable loot and let his comrades continue the pursuit by themselves. But this contradicts all sensible military practice, since it is necessary above all to make the most of victory and do as much damage to the enemy as one can, and for this purpose all the men must be kept together. So Nestor, experienced in war, calls to the Argives with his resounding voice, Z 68ff.:

[I.47]

μή τις νῦν ἐνάρων ἐπιβαλλόμενος μετόπισθεν
μιμνέτω, ὥς κεν πλεῖστα φέρων ἐπὶ νῆας ἵκηται,
ἀλλ᾽ ἄνδρας κτείνωμεν· ἔπειτα δὲ καὶ τὰ ἕκηλοι
νεκροὺς ἂμ πεδίον συλήσετε τεθνηῶτας.

'No looting now! No lingering behind to get back to the ships with the biggest share! Let us kill Trojans. Afterwards, at your leisure, you can strip the dead on the battlefield.'

Again, in O 347ff., Hector, who was to an even greater extent obliged to exploit the favourable turn that the war had finally taken with a view to the complete annihilation of the enemy and the capture of the ships, threatens his men who want to pick up booty during the pursuit and shouts as follows: 'On to the Greek ships! Forget about seizing the bloodstained loot! Anyone I see hanging back, I'll kill him on the spot. The dogs will tear his body in front of Ilium.'

Since Helenus fears that the Trojans in their demoralised state, Z 74, may flee right back to the city, he persuades Hector and Aeneas first to halt the rout and then to engage in a 'standing battle' hard up against the walls of the city until Hector has organised the procession of the Trojan women to appeal to Athene at her temple. Hector jumps off his chariot, – verse 80 clearly shows that both heroes are again in front of the fleeing men: στῆτ᾽ αὐτοῦ καὶ λαὸν ἐρυκάκετε πρὸ πυλάων *make a stand here* and *halt* the troops in front of the gates' – and the flight comes to a stop. So it was not the command of a god this time but only the word of the seer Helenus which brought about the sudden change. But it is extremely typical when the poet comments, 108, that the Achaeans gave way in astonishment at the sudden about-turn of the Trojans,

φὰν δέ τιν᾽ ἀθανάτων ἐξ οὐρανοῦ ἀστερόεντος
Τρωσὶν ἀλεξήσοντα κατελθέμεν, ὡς ἐλέλιχθεν.

'They thought *some god* must have come down from the starry sky to *help the Trojans*, so effectively did they rally'.

We have already briefly discussed the flight of the Achaeans, H 15-

18, which is caused by the re-intervention of Hector and Paris and only sketched in a few words.

On the second day of battle, after the fight had fluctuated for a long time, Zeus caused panic in the Achaean lines, Θ 77, so that all the heroes took flight and could not be halted even by Diomedes' brave advance. In the narrow space between ditch and wall infantry and chariots were penned together in a confused mêlée, all filled with a blind fear of Hector, 215-16. Again, it is a sign of support sent by Zeus, visible to all, that brings about the change, 251. Suddenly all the Greeks are thinking of battle again, and Diomedes is the first to turn his chariot to attack the pursuers. The first victim of his spear is Agelaus who has naturally outpaced the Trojan infantry on his chariot during the pursuit; but now he has turned his horses to flight again and, hit in the back, falls off his chariot, 257-60. Among the other Greek leaders Teucer particularly distinguishes himself, fighting on foot, as also is Ajax, 271-2. This time Hector has not driven ahead of the Trojans in flight with his swift horses, 299, 322 (anyway, they are pictured as retreating slowly rather than fleeing at speed); indeed Teucer regards it as necessary to hide behind Ajax's shield after every shot, 271-2. Then Hector jumps off his chariot to go against Teucer, whom he puts out of action with a stone throw, 320ff. After this, Zeus again inspires the Trojans with courage for battle, 335, and ahead of everyone else Hector now pursues the Greeks who are in panic flight back to the ditch, always killing the hindmost. In so doing, he himself so captures the spotlight that, even though the rest of the Trojans with him are also imagined as striking at the Greeks, 344, Hera says that the Achaeans are dying ἀνδρὸς ἑνὸς ῥιπῇ 'by one man's onslaught', 355. At the beginning of the pursuit he had mounted his chariot again, 348, and only nightfall puts an end to it, 485ff.

[I.48] On the third day of battle also, the fight at first remains in the balance for a long time until the bravery of the Achaeans succeeds in breaking through the lines of the Trojans, σφῇ ἀρετῇ Δαναοὶ ῥήξαντο φάλαγγας 'the Greeks summoned up their courage and broke the enemy lines', Λ 90. The rout begins immediately and Agamemnon storms ahead of all others into the lines of the Trojans and kills Bienor together with his driver Oileus, who had jumped off the chariot in vain to help his comrade. This first pair of victims is followed immediately by the pair of brothers Isus and Antiphus, εἰν ἑνὶ δίφρῳ ἑόντας 'who were on a single chariot' 103; and immediately after them another pair, also standing on one chariot, 127, Peisander and Hippolochus, after the reins had slipped out of the latter's hand and the horses had bolted. Agamemnon had easily caught up with them in consequence and, in spite of their tearful entreaties, strikes them down with spear and sword. So these are very similar scenes to those which coloured the picture of wild panic in Diomedes' *aristeia*, and this also seems to me to be typical, that the most celebrated exploits of these outstanding Greek heroes are performed not in battle against the resistance of a brave opponent, but during the rout of an enemy fleeing in disorder. So too the other Greeks, like Agamemnon, leapt on the fleeing Trojans and killed anyone they could catch, τῇ ῥ' ἐνόρουσ', ἅμα δ' ἄλλοι ἐϋκνήμιδες Ἀχαιοί, 'he dashed in there, and with him the other well-greaved Achaeans', 149, 150-4. And again and again it is emphasised afresh how Agamemnon pursues the fleeing, helpless Trojans, 153, 165, 168, 178; and the picture of this hopeless confusion is presented to us in ever new colours, 155-62: they have been utterly torn apart, and only under the protection of the walls do they dare halt their desperate run and await their comrades who are being hunted across the plain and slaughtered like cattle attacked by a lion, 171ff. Deliverance, again, only comes through the intervention of Zeus, who sends Iris to Hector with instructions to restore the battle line and himself to keep away from the fighting until Agamemnon is wounded, 204ff. This happens, 214, the Achaeans also re-form their ranks which had been scattered by the pursuit, and a new battle begins, 215. But as soon as Hector has noticed that Agamemnon has been driven from the battle wounded, he, assured of victory by Zeus' promise, calls upon the Trojans for a strong forward push, and indeed with the rather surprising words (289): ἰθὺς ἐλαύνετε μώνυχας ἵππους ἰφθίμων Δαναῶν 'Drive your horses straight at the warlike Greeks'. One almost feels tempted to regard these words as a pointer to the flight and pursuit of the Greeks, which begin immediately; for, without having described a battle, the poet immediately presents us with a picture of the Achaeans, all order gone, in wild flight, hunted down by Hector, 299ff. Only Greek heroes fall, and after the Greek leaders – otherwise quite unknown names – have been killed, the πληθύς 'common crowd' is butchered by Hector *en masse*, without resistance, 305. The Achaeans would have fled in disorder all the way to the ships without stopping, 311, if Odysseus and Diomedes had not gone into action against the pursuers to hold them up and give the fleeing men some breathing space, 327.

When at the beginning of M the poet has the Trojan leaders appear on their chariots and then dismount at the ditch with the aim of storming the wall, he keeps to the existing situation exactly, since the Trojans were engaged in the pursuit of the Danaans who were crowded together Διὸς μάστιγι δαμέντες 'cowed by Zeus' scourge', 37. But in the same way it corresponds to this state of affairs when later, Ξ 506ff., during the wild rout brought about by Poseidon – ἔκλινε μάχην κλυτὸς ἐννοσίγαιος 'the famous earthshaker swayed the battle' 510 –

the poet has them all on foot and emphasises expressly that Ajax, Oileus' son, killed the most Trojans (and only Trojan warriors fall, 511ff.) because nobody was his equal in speed of foot, 521; for before the beginning of the battle for the Greek ships the chariots of the Trojans had remained back at the ditch, something of which we are expressly reminded, O 3.

I have earlier discussed the **[I.49]** sudden turn of the battle brought about by Apollo's intervention and Hector's unexpected appearance in the fighting, and the attempt at a rearguard action, O 279ff.; I will just add, in connection with the other flight scenes, that here, too, during the Trojan pursuit only Greek heroes fall, 329ff. The Trojan leaders appear on their chariots, 352-4, and in order to enable them to make an effective pursuit right up to the ships – since Zeus' command to Apollo, 233, was to this effect – Apollo has levelled the ditch to the width of a spear-throw, 358. The god himself strides ahead on foot, and the majority of the Trojans are imagined as doing the same – it is said of them, 360, τῇ ῥ' οἵ γε προχέοντο φαλαγγηδόν 'here they poured across rank after rank'. Only when they reach the ships do the Achaeans regroup, encouraging each other, and, protecting the threatened ships, put up resistance to the Trojans so that the latter cannot break through their ranks, 409. In the battle which then begins the leaders have again left their chariots.

The brilliant description of the Trojans' wild flight after the intervention of the Myrmidons under Patroclus, which develops from a fighting retreat, Π 278ff., is also made clear and vivid by the simplest means. When the Trojans, who have been victorious so far, see Patroclus storming towards them with his feared company of warriors, they lose courage and their lines begin to waver, 280; Patroclus hurls his spear into the middle of the throng, and the Trojans retreat from Protesilaus' ship which is already on fire; then the Danaans storm forward in other parts of the battlefield as well, 295, and the withdrawal of the Trojans becomes more general. But not yet προτροπάδην φοβέοντο 'were they in headlong flight' 304; resistance is still put up here and there, and this is expressly recalled in the enumeration of the fallen Trojans, 319, 335; furthermore, the Trojans have not yet mounted their chariots and only Meriones hits Acamas κιχεὶς ποσὶ καρπαλίμοισι 'using his speed to catch him' 342, when he is just about to climb on to his chariot. The flight becomes more and more general, 356-7; Hector alone stays his ground, although he sees that all is lost, and slowly retreats from the enemy to cover the withdrawal of his men, 359-63. Finally he too jumps on to his chariot and, carried by his swift horses, hurries far ahead of his fleeing men, and the Trojan army rushes after him, scattered across the whole plain and dissolved in wild flight and utter confusion, 374. Now Patroclus tries above all to catch up with Hector, 382, and therefore drives after his opponent, who is galloping away from him, through the ranks of the fleeing Trojans; by doing this he, like the fleeing Hector, comes to be in front of the foremost ranks of the Trojan foot-soldiers, whom he cuts off, 394, and drives back to the ships, barring their way to the city, 395. This is the only way I can understand πρώτας ἐπέκερσε φάλαγγας 'cut off the first Trojan contingents' 394, and I cannot agree with the explanation of Ameis and Düntzer who want to interpret them as 'the most advanced ranks of the fleeing men, who had therefore stood nearest the ships before and were now the closest to the pursuing Patroclus'.

Then Patroclus leaps off his chariot, cf. Ameis on 398, and rages devastatingly among the fleeing ranks; only Trojans are named as having been killed on this occasion, 394-418. Only through Sarpedon's undaunted intervention is the victorious enemy halted; later Glaucus, who thanks to Apollo's miraculous help has been healed and filled with new courage, 529, even succeeds in persuading the Lycians, and then the Trojans too, to protect Sarpedon's corpse. The flight generally comes to a halt; the scattered contingents are regrouped on both sides, 563, and with a loud battle cry they engage in a fight for the corpse of the brave prince of the Lycians, 565ff. Of the general flight of the Trojans which is then brought about by the will of Zeus (Hector, filled with fear, had mounted his chariot and ordered his men to follow him, 657) I only mention as important for our question that at the beginning of the pursuit Patroclus tells his chariot driver to drive after him and advances on foot himself, 685, cf. Ameis, and that the list of casualties in 692-7 again contains none but Trojan names; τοὺς ἕλεν, οἱ δ᾽ ἄλλοι φύγαδε μνώοντο ἕκαστος 'these he killed; all the rest turned to flight', 697.

[I.50] The verses which now follow, 698-711, in which the victorious Patroclus puts his foot on the walls of Troy, but is pushed back by Apollo, are quite incompatible with the subsequent description, presenting him to us still on his chariot in pursuit of the Trojans. Without going into this question in detail here, I regard them as a clumsy later addition in every case. In brief, characteristic strokes verses 712ff. continue the description of flight and pursuit: Hector has outpaced his men in flight, but on Apollo's advice drives at the victorious Patroclus again. His chariot driver is killed, and a duel on foot results and then a general fight for the corpse of Cebriones, quite similar to the previous one for that of Sarpedon, only here the whole scene has been shifted a step closer to Troy.

The passage P 597ff. also is very typical of the poet's method of description of which numerous examples have been given. Here we are dealing with the flight of the whole Greek army, brought about by Zeus, who shakes his aegis, creating a mighty thunderstorm around

Ida, νίκην δὲ Τρώεσσι δίδου, ἐφόβησε δ᾽ Ἀχαιούς 'and gave victory to the Trojans and filled the Greeks with panic' 596; but the general flight is described only in one typical scene. It was Peneleos who ἦρχε φόβοιο 'was the first to turn and run'; Polydamas had wounded him σχεδὸν ἐλθών 'coming up to him at short range', and Hector had likewise hit Leïtus σχεδὸν 'at close range'; now as Hector leaps after Leïtus, Idomeneus launches a spear at him, 605, but the spear shatters on Hector's armour; but the next moment, when Hector wants to return the shot, Idomeneus has already jumped on to Meriones' chariot, 609, as a third person, since Meriones' chariot driver Coeranus had arrived to take him up; this was lucky for Idomeneus, who had come on foot from the ships into battle. Coeranus himself has to lose his life for this loyal deed, since the spear meant for Idomeneus hits him. Now Meriones from the chariot immediately picks up the reins which had fallen to the ground, 620, and they both hasten away to the ships.[19] So great was their haste that three of them had wanted to escape on one chariot; and the fact that this hurried flight was general is confirmed by the words used at Σ 148, where the description is resumed after the interruption caused by the sending of Antilochus: αὐτὰρ Ἀχαιοὶ θεσπεσίῳ ἀλαλητῷ ὑφ᾽ Ἕκτορος ἀνδροφόνοιο φεύγοντες νῆας ... ἵκοντο 'meanwhile the Greeks, running with cries of terror from man-slaying Hector, streamed back to the ships'.

Also, in the picture of confused flight which the poet presents to us after Achilles' return to the fray, Υ 381ff., which still requires a brief mention, the same features present themselves, even though Achilles stands almost on his own in the foreground. With the armies facing each other, 373-4, Achilles had leapt into the middle of the Trojans, and the enemy now killed by him are listed initially in rather leisurely sequence, and with some Trojans still reported as putting up resistance, 400, – Hector too makes an attempt at fighting him, 419ff. – then, 455ff., the men killed follow in swifter succession: a pair of brothers on a chariot, 460, many others slaughtered now with the sword, now with the spear, Rhigmus together with his chariot driver who had just turned the horses to flight, 486. Finally Achilles himself appears on his chariot, pursuing the fleeing Trojans over the corpses of the dead up to the Scamander. After he has killed Asteropaeus in the river, he mercilessly slaughters the latter's men, Φ 209ff.; indeed, he kills horses and men 521, οὐδέ τις ἀλκὴ γίγνεθ᾽ 'and there was no resistance' (528). On other occasions the protecting walls of the city had always brought the disorderly flight to an end, and it had been possible by keeping close to them to gather the dispersed contingents and regroup them for renewed resistance, but now everyone was thinking only about his own skin, as the final verses of Φ vividly describe, 608ff.:

οὐδ᾽ ἄρα τοί γ᾽ ἔτλαν πόλιος καὶ τείχεος ἐκτὸς
μεῖναι ἔτ᾽ ἀλλήλους καὶ γνώμεναι ὅς τε πεφεύγοι [I.51]
ὅς τ᾽ ἔθαν᾽ ἐν πολέμῳ· ἀλλ᾽ ἐσσυμένως ἐσέχυντο
ἐς πόλιν, ὅν τινα τῶν γε πόδες καὶ γοῦνα σαώσαι.

'They did not even have the spirit *to wait for each other* outside the town walls in order to find out who had got away or who had fallen in battle. Instead, those whose speed of foot had saved them *poured eagerly into the town.*'

For, in order to let them in, Priam had had the Scaean Gate opened, 530ff. This was of course a very dangerous way of helping. How easily could the pursuer force his way into the city among the helpless fugitives, cf. X 1ff. – and then they would all be done for. No Trojan hero any more has the heart to make a courageous advance which would, even for a short time, have held up the victorious enemy. So it is a god who has to step into the breach here to help and take on the function which, on other occasions during flight, one or several brave heroes had never failed to fulfil, Φ 538: Ἀπόλλων ἀντίος ἐξέθορε, Τρώων ἵνα λοιγὸν ἀλάλκοι 'Apollo *rushed out to meet the threat* and avert disaster from the Trojans'. He rescues the helpless Trojans by diverting Achilles away from the threatened gate, first through Agenor, then himself taking on the appearance of Agenor.

These attempts by brave heroes to face their pursuer and delay him for a time by a short but spirited attack have been repeatedly referred to in the preceding discussions, so that a brief reminder is surely sufficient at this point. We certainly should regard this action, which appears almost regularly in all descriptions of flight, as taken from real life; not, of course, that one individual hero would be able to stop a whole victorious army, but certainly in the sense that a number of determined heroes who now here, now there, turn and make a stand from among the fleeing troops and show the enemy their teeth, can without doubt provide effective protection for their hard-pressed comrades. Precisely for this reason it seems to me absolutely typical of the panic which the poet wishes to attribute to the Trojans in their flight from the victorious Achilles, that he does not allow any of them to rise to such an act of bravery and self-sacrifice. The main passages relevant to our question are, briefly, the following: Ε 166 during the general flight of the Trojans, Aeneas goes to Pandarus to join him in facing Diomedes, 218: πάρος δ᾽ οὐκ ἔσσεται ἄλλως, πρίν γ᾽ ἐπὶ νὼ τῷδ᾽ ἀνδρὶ σὺν ἵπποισιν καὶ ὄχεσφιν ἀντιβίην ἐλθόντε σὺν ἔντεσι πειρηθῆναι 'Things are not going to change till you and I confront him in full armour from a chariot and find out what he's made of'. Their bravery is successful in that, for a while, a 'standing battle' develops for the supposed corpse of Aeneas. With the same intention, and to even better effect,

Athene and Diomedes drive at the Trojans, Ε 837ff., and put Ares, their mightiest helper, out of action. On the second day of battle, when everyone else flees, Θ 78ff., Diomedes remains behind the Greeks with his chariot, and after vainly encouraging Odysseus, who is dashing past him at speed, to be brave, 93: Ὀδυσσεῦ, πῇ φεύγεις μετὰ νῶτα βαλών, κακὸς ὣς ἐν ὁμίλῳ 'Odysseus, where are you off to, *turning your back* like a coward in the crowd?', he drives on his own to help out Nestor who is under pressure and subsequently with Nestor against Hector. Diomedes is filled with such courage that he needs forcibly to be reminded several times by Zeus' flash of lightning that this is not the time for such daring, and that the old fellow on Olympus has other plans. A similar staying back behind the lines, which incidentally can and should occur also nowadays among individual units in a retreat, was mentioned by us above, Π 363, in relation to Hector, who still held out when the flight was becoming more general, σάω δ' ἐρίηρας ἑταίρους 'and tried to save his loyal men'. Later, 727ff., urged by Apollo, Hector drove up to fight the pursuing Patroclus, just as previously it had been Sarpedon, 419ff., who had turned his chariot round and lost his life in the fight with Patroclus, trying to support his desperately hard-pressed comrades.

It was, of course, far more dangerous and less likely to succeed to go and face the victorious pursuers on foot, as Diomedes and Odysseus dare to do in Λ 312ff. The Greeks were in wildest flight from Hector and ἔνθα κε λοιγὸς ἔην καὶ ἀμήχανα **[I.52]** ἔργα γένοντο 'irreparable disaster now threatened them', if Odysseus had not called on Diomedes to go over to the offensive again to save the ships, τί παθόντε λελάσμεθα θούριδος ἀλκῆς; 'What's the matter with us? Where's that *fighting spirit* of ours gone?' Diomedes declares that, despite the bad situation, he is ready to make a stand, and they kill a number of Trojans, first among them being Thymbraeus who was pursuing by chariot, together with his driver, 320ff. The positive success of their intervention is expressly emphasised, 327: αὐτὰρ Ἀχαιοὶ ἀσπασίως φεύγοντες ἀνέπνεον Ἕκτορα δῖον 'they gave the Greeks *a welcome pause for breath in their flight* from god-like Hector'. But it was particularly dangerous for a hero to stay behind when he did not even have his chariot near him. Separated far from his fleeing comrades, how easily could he be surrounded and cut off! Then it was a matter of fighting his way out or having himself rescued by loyal friends, an event which was surely not uncommon; and here too, Λ 401ff., it is described to us by the poet with graphic vividness. After his wounding, Diomedes had driven to the ships and – not very comradely – left Odysseus on his own. While the latter is still deliberating whether he should flee or stay and is considering in particular the danger of being cut off, 405, the Trojans, on foot and in chariots, as they were during the pursuit, crowd in upon the courageous hero. Many are killed by him, and they all clearly keep themselves at a respectful distance from the dangerous tip of his spear; but they do not let him out either, just as hunters and hounds keep an encircled boar surrounded, which, attacking with its tusks, threatens anyone who dares approach. Only Socus, provoked by his brother's death, goes up close and wounds him right through his shield, but flees hastily when Odysseus, in spite of his injury, goes for him, 446. But when they see the hero's blood flowing, the other Trojans grow more courageous and crowd in upon the hard-pressed hero in denser throngs. Odysseus has to retreat and, in urgent danger of being completely cut off, shouts loudly for help. Then Ajax and Menelaus undertake to rescue their comrade in great danger (467-8: ὡς εἴ ἑ βιῴατο μοῦνον ἐόντα Τρῶες ἀποτμήξαντες ἐνὶ κρατερῇ ὑσμίνῃ, 'it sounds as though the Trojans have cut him off in the thick of the action') and carry out their intention in the most skilful manner. Both advance, with the chariot following them, while Odysseus holds the closely surrounding Trojans at bay with his spear, 484. Then mighty Ajax suddenly leaps straight at the circle of Trojans, who scatter in all directions in terror, 486. Menelaus exploits this favourable moment, leads Odysseus out of the tumult to the swiftly approaching chariot, and, under the cover of brave Ajax who holds off the Trojans with great success, they climb in and are driven off, 488.

The degree of success which Ajax then achieves, 489ff., esp. 497, must however surprise us, even if Hector does not participate in the fight, 497, because he had only advanced to rescue Odysseus, as much as the fear which suddenly overtakes him, 544, and his withdrawal which would actually have fitted much better had it immediately followed the rescue of Odysseus. Hentze, *Appendix*, Introduction, has referred to other reservations that are brought against this passage; what was of interest for our enquiry was, above all, the method by which the encircled Odysseus is rescued.

But I have to stop here so as not to exceed too much the limits of space allowed me. Of course many other points remain to be discussed in order to complete an investigation of warfare in Homeric time; in particular, I have not been able to touch at all on the questions of safeguarding one's army in enemy territory, of attacking a fortified camp (which was by now a familiar situation), and of the art of attacking fortified cities (still in its infancy). Perhaps these may be discussed in detail on another occasion.

Notes

1. For discussion of the meaning of the term translated by Albracht *stehendes Gefecht* 'standing fight', see Appendix, p. 139; it is very common in this

work (cf. 18, 21, 29, etc.) and is the title of the section beginning on p. 53.

2. Albracht is of his age, and believes that apparent inconsistencies in the text of the *Iliad* can be explained by the assumption of multiple authorship (the view of the 'Analysts', dominant in Germany at that time and for long after). However, as he says, his arguments gain in simplicity if they are presented as conditionally referring to a single author, whom we call Homer.

3. The apocryphal ancient *Life of Homer* attributed to Herodotus alleges that Homer lived as a schoolmaster on the island of Chios (vol. 5 of the Oxford text of Homer, ed. T.W. Allen, p. 207, section 25).

4. Albracht calls it (here and elsewhere) a 'phalanx', a term which we have decided not to use. See Appendix, p. 139.

5. For discussion of the term πρόμαχοι, 'front line fighters', frequently found in Homer's battle scenes, see Appendix, p. 139.

6. N 131-3 = Π 215-17, discussed on pp. 66-7.

7. See pp. 79-81.

8. Cf. Hentze, ad loc.

9. See Diomedes at Θ 104, Nestor at Ψ 309-10.

10. This is a new interpretation of the phrase; see Janko ad loc. ('victory with the help of others'). The traditional explanation (which would have been shared by Albracht himself) was that Hector recognised that the victory was with the side which had previously been losing.

11. Cf. n. 1.

12. See Appendix, p. 139.

13. Idomeneus was grey-haired, N 361.

14. The references to the *Iliad* scholia here and on p. 67 are to Bekker's edition (Berlin, 1825), which preceded that of Dindorf and Maas (1877-87), which itself has now been superseded by Erbse (1969-88).

15. In 1386, at the battle of Sempach in Switzerland between the Swiss confederation and the Austrian knights under Leopold III, Arnold Winkelried, on the Swiss side, by a heroic act of self-sacrifice created a gap in the enemy line, which was used by his comrades to gain the victory.

16. For the scholia, see n. 14. The 'paraphrase' is found in what are called the Scholia Minora, or D Scholia, quoted in Bekker, but not in Erbse.

17. The assumption in the *Iliad* is that shields were made of several thicknesses of ox-hide. Ajax's was seven hides thick. These are called πτύχες 'folds', e.g. at H 247.

18. On p. 31.

19. This is a rare error by Albracht, repeated in later writers. As the text makes clear, Meriones stays to fight, but sends his superior, Idomeneus, to safety out of the battle. The authoritative commentators Ameis-Henze and Faesi-Franke describe the situation rightly.

Part II

Introduction

[II.1] At the end of my *Battle and Battle Description in Homer*, which appeared in 1886 as a supplement to the annual report of the State School Pforta, I expressed the hope that I would be able to complete my investigation on another occasion and reach some conclusions about the questions not yet settled. In attempting to conclude the discussion in the present treatise, I hope to offer something that will be welcomed by many of the friends and admirers of Homer, and here again to make a small contribution to the interpretation and understanding of the poet. The point of view from which I approach the investigation is principally still the same as in the first part. Homer is a poet and not a military historian (whose main priority would consist in presenting tactical ideas, developing the art of strategy and solving difficult problems of battle and war). The poet and his audience, on the other hand, derive pleasure from the description of military actions, even if it were just the delight and pride they feel in the great feats of their fathers; they have an understanding of battle and war and of the means by which victory is forced and through which peace (which, in spite of all innate bravery and heroic courage, is still more beautiful) is won. They are, like the poet himself presumably – and again, for simplicity's sake, I ask to be allowed to speak throughout of *the* poet[1] – not without their own experience in battle and war and can, so to speak, act as a control on the poet, just as we today can still act as a control on his depictions of nature and of the feelings of the human heart, which are observed with such masterly refinement. Only depictions of the events of war which are built on truth, on real life, can inspire the poet's contemporaries, secure immortality for the singer of heroic songs, create a Homer. So, even if the military side of things is not in itself the purpose and goal of his narrative, it is still to an outstanding degree the means to his end. When he wants vividly to depict the brave deeds of a hero or a tribe under the leadership of its prince, e.g. the Trojans' assault on the Greek wall, he, the master of clarity, can do this only by having the leaders and men involved resort to those means, take those steps, which were known at that time and which competent leaders and brave soldiers would usually take in such cases. But he could never invent from his imagination and vividly describe a walled fortification with its individual features – a ditch with palisade, a proper attack on it and its carefully planned defence – if all this was not already known from real life, any more than he describes to us from his imagination a Greek assault on the walled city of Troy with ladders and battering-rams, the construction of a surrounding wall, the starving out of the fortress, or has his mighty heroes (who, of course, put whole armies to flight and are not even afraid of the gods) climb over the walls of the fortress of Troy, force open its gates or have the walls knocked down, perhaps with the help of the gods (which would have been a small matter for a Hephaestus or Poseidon's trident), because such feats of war were still completely unknown to him and to the heroes of his time, nor were such means yet used for the capture of a city.

[II.2] Virgil, on the other hand, who truly cannot compete with Homer in the understanding of and interest in the events of war, describes rams and ladders being used as a matter of course in the storming of the royal palace in Troy, because they were familiar for this purpose among the Romans of his time, and everybody would have been surprised if they had not been used for capturing a fortified and well defended building. Examples from a whole series of poetic compositions, whose content refers to battle and war through the Middle Ages up until the most recent time, could easily be adduced to show by examples the obvious fact that they clearly reflect advances in weaponry as well as in tactics, and that, in these questions, poetic imagination reflects the sober reality of practical life.

So the description of tactical measures to achieve the goal which was striven for in battle was not Homer's object, but only the means of illustration and dramatisation which came to him more or less automatically. His audience had to have the feeling – 'yes, this is how it was done,' 'this is what happens in battle,' 'this is how we have experienced it ourselves,' or 'this is how an intelligent leader had to act.' Whether the events themselves which are described correspond to the facts in every respect is a quite minor matter, but they must not leave the realm of the possible; they must always remain natural. When individual heroes, or gods taking part in the battle, accomplish something unusually marvellous, the action may indeed exceed the norms of human ability, but it never crosses the boundaries of what was common knowledge of military matters possessed by ordinary people of that time. The base-line remains the same, and is only to some extent elevated when compared with human achievements; the parameters of the art of war as known at the time are not crossed. Nor do the gods, in *their* battles, show any advances in the sphere of arms and of battle tactics in the open field or against a fortified city.

If therefore in our investigation we completely disregard the artistic aims of the poet, and merely restrict ourselves to enquiring into the means by which he makes his descriptions vivid and breathes such fresh, joyful life into them that even today we still feel his pulse beat warmly, if we, so to speak, detach these means (i.e. the assumptions behind the convincing descriptions of battle) from the narrative itself and look at them in isolation, we certainly find ourselves on real, firm, ground and do not float on mere clouds of poetic imagination. If, on the other hand, we admit quite unreservedly that the poet creates for himself the situations as he needs them for his purposes, we must nevertheless keep firmly in our minds that he creates for himself only natural, possible situations which have been taken from real life and could be transposed back into it, which have life and are not mere figments of his imagination.

Homer and his contemporaries obviously took a particular delight in the description of events of war. We understand this from the devoted care with which the battles are represented with all their details and in all the different ways imaginable. In all Homer's descriptions, one comes to an understanding in the quickest, most penetrating and most certain way if one tries to imagine the situation described from all sides, in as it were a three-dimensional way; so too his battle descriptions are most carefully composed – not, of course, each individual battle scene on its own (that would become intolerably tedious), but in such a way that, from the sum of all the battle descriptions, we learn virtually all the particular details we could ask for, and from them can, on the whole, construct for ourselves a well-ordered and clear picture of the course of events. Just as we gain in this way quite a clear understanding of the course of a battle in Homeric time from the representation of the different types of fighting in the open field – the σταδίη μάχη 'standing fight', the massed attack, the **[II.3]** fighting retreat, flight and pursuit, and the incidents, scenes and events typical of them, in the same way we can get a reasonably clear picture of other undertakings in the military life of that time – protecting one's camp against the enemy, attacking a fortification, siege and defence of a walled city – by using the method indicated above in regard to the poet's descriptions; and, from the knowledge of war which he assumes to be familiar and universal, we can construct for ourselves a picture of the art of warfare of his time in its most important aspects. We shall first discuss:

Protection Against the Enemy

Once the decision to besiege a fortified city had been taken, the besieging army, which, with its crowd of camp-followers, itself resembled a small city, had naturally to take measures to make itself at home as much as possible by building huts and safeguarding the whole of the living accommodation to the best of its ability against destruction from possible enemy attacks. One could not live on board ship for any length of time, and the kings and princes of that time had to content themselves with very simply furnished cabins in which they would certainly not stay any longer than the duration of the sea voyage absolutely required. Then huts, κλισίαι, were built on the shore, somewhat bigger ones for the princes, since they had various kinds of representative functions and tended to create for themselves a complete household with a greater or lesser number of female slaves, smaller ones for the soldiers, but still all of them indicating that extended occupation was expected. The mildness of the climate – it is characteristic that in the *Iliad* a difference of seasons is never mentioned in relation to the siege and the buildings connected with it – and the simplicity which has always to prevail in a military camp made the whole matter of accommodation very much easier. Nevertheless, the camp was valuable and essential enough; indeed, it was a requirement for the continued existence of the army and the prosecution of the siege, and as a result it was necessary to give it the maximum protection. The fact that Homer makes the Greeks fortify their camp only in the tenth year of the siege is, of course, poetic licence, by which, as is well known, he likes to allow his audience to witness such important things for themselves. We can be certain of this: the Greeks who besieged Troy fortified their camp soon after landing, when by a victory they had made themselves masters of the sea shore, (Thuc. I 11 ἐπειδὴ δὲ ἀφικόμενοι μάχῃ ἐκράτησαν, δῆλον δέ· τὸ γὰρ ἔρυμα τῷ στρατοπέδῳ οὐκ ἂν ἐτειχίσαντο, 'when they arrived they won a victory. The evidence is that the fortifications for their camp could not otherwise have been built'). They did so with the means which were at their disposal, and protected it against hostile attacks.

Now, what are those means? Let us first follow the poet, who brings the camp into existence before our eyes.

In H 338ff. Nestor, οὗ καὶ πρόσθεν ἀρίστη φαίνετο βουλή 'whose wisdom had often proved itself in the past' (325) proposes to the princes in the assembly – and it is typical that here again, as on other occasions, a measure demanded by the general situation and the military practices of the time appears as a new proposal of the old Pylian – δείμομεν ὦκα / πύργους ὑψηλούς, εἶλαρ νηῶν τε καὶ αὐτῶν. / ἐν δ᾽ αὐτοῖσι πύλας ποιήσομεν εὖ ἀραρυίας, / ὄφρα δι᾽ αὐτάων ἱππηλασίη ὁδὸς εἴη. / ἔκτοσθεν δὲ βαθεῖαν ὀρύξομεν ἐγγύθι τάφρον, / ἥ χ᾽ ἵππους καὶ λαὸν ἐρυκάκοι ἀμφὶς ἐοῦσα, / μή ποτ᾽ ἐπιβρίσῃ πόλεμος Τρώων ἀγερώχων, 'We should immediately construct high-towered walls to protect the ships and ourselves, and well-fitted gates in them, that leave room for chariots to drive through. And outside the wall we should dig a deep ditch nearby to keep out enemy chariots and infantry, in case the proud Trojans start putting the pressure on us some day.' Nestor's proposal meets with general approval, and so presumably also understanding, in the assembly, 344, and is carried out the next day as lines 436-41 inform us in the same words.

[II.4] Since the Greeks plan to build πύργους ὑψηλούς 'high towers' for the protection of the ships, and it is said of these in the following verse: ἐν δ' αὐτοῖσι πύλας ποιήσομεν ... ὄφρα δι' αὐτάων ἱππηλασίη ὁδὸς εἴη 'we should construct gates in them that leave room for chariots to drive through', we should for a start imagine this route as arched over, rather than leading through a free standing gate. Ameis explains 'a wall with towers', certainly quite correctly, but we must not imagine these towers to be like those of the later art of fortification and siege, particularly the Roman. The πύργοι 'towers' of the Greek camp do not rise substantially above the height of the wall, as the ensuing descriptions of the battle fought for them show. As our passage already indicates, they serve mainly for the protection of the gates, which are most under threat during an attack, and are therefore built on both sides of these, cf. 339: ἐν δ' αὐτοῖσι πύλας ποιήσομεν 'we should construct gates in them'. If they are the same height as the wall, they are (more or less) just widened and enlarged locations on it, suitable for holding a larger number of defenders on the upper level, and from this it can be understood that the word πύργος 'tower' is used almost synonymously with τεῖχος 'wall'. As exits and entrances for the foot-soldiers, the πύλαι 'gates' of a camp could be quite narrow because the battle-line is drawn up only outside the camp, and their strength and defensibility would gain much as a result, but the chariots which drive the leaders to the mustering-place and into battle must be able to pass through, ἱππηλασίη ὁδός 'a road wide enough for chariots to drive through', and therefore a double gate must be employed, M 121, 459-61. However, the number of chariots in the Greek camp was small, and one main gate sufficed for their traffic. Perhaps that is the reason why, with the exception of a few passages, H 339, 438, M 120, 175, 340, only one gate is always mentioned in the Greek camp.

The material for the wall was of course obtained on site, and we must not imagine the building to have been all that flimsy, even though Zeus advises Poseidon, H 461, simply to wash the whole wall away into the sea; for when this destruction is being carried out, M 17ff., the two gods direct all the rivers of the Ida mountain range against it, and make these masses of water do their work for nine days until everything has again been covered by sand. Here we learn that they first had to wash away all the foundations which the Greeks had laboriously laid from beams and stones, M 28-9: ἐκ δ' ἄρα πάντα θεμείλια κύμασι πέμπε / φιτρῶν καὶ λάων, τὰ θέσαν μογέοντες Ἀχαιοί 'he washed out to sea all the wooden and stone footings that the Greeks had laid with such labour'.

We shall come to individual features which are meant to increase the defensibility of the wall when we discuss the battle for it, but I would just like to add here the statement N 683 that the wall had been built at its lowest by the ships of Ajax[2] and Protesilaus, αὐτὰρ ὕπερθε / τεῖχος ἐδέδμητο χθαμαλώτατον 'there the wall had been built at its lowest'. This should probably just be regarded as a compliment to the bravery of the two heroes. Nor is it surprising that some stretches of the wall offered the enemy more accessible points of attack than others, and their defence might very well be the continuing responsibility of the bravest heroes.

In front of the wall, Η 440-1, the Greeks dug a ditch βαθεῖαν, εὐρεῖαν, μεγάλην, ἐν δὲ σκόλοπας κατέπηξαν 'deep, broad and long, and planted a row of stakes along it'. Naturally, the poet has the Greeks make their ditch deep and broad, since these are the basis of the protection it affords; with μεγάλην 'long' the great length is indicated, corresponding to the length of the camp wall, and the σκόλοπες 'stakes' put in at the side also increase its security. But where is the ditch dug and where are the σκόλοπες 'stakes' fixed? At first sight, it appears most natural to suppose that the ditch is close to the wall, so that the excavated earth could be immediately used for its construction. The expressions Η 341 ὀρύξομεν ἐγγύθι τάφρον 'we should dig a ditch nearby' and Η 440 ἐπ' αὐτῷ τάφρον ὄρυξαν 'they dug a ditch beside it' also seem to indicate this, whereas Η 449 τεῖχος ἐτειχίσσαντο, ... ἀμφὶ δὲ τάφρον ἤλασαν 'they have built a wall ... and dug a ditch along it' or Μ 5 τάφρος ... καὶ τεῖχος ὕπερθεν / εὐρύ, τὸ ποιήσαντο νεῶν ὕπερ, ἀμφὶ δὲ τάφρον / ἤλασαν 'the ditch ... and the wide wall above it which they made to protect the ships, and they dug a ditch along it' **[II.5]** leave this question undecided. On the other hand, a series of other passages definitely assume a considerable space between wall and ditch. I list a few of these first in order to complete the picture of the Greek camp.

In Θ 177ff., after even the brave Diomedes has turned his back, the Greeks are in full flight from the pursuing Trojans. The poet says of them in 213 τῶν δ' ὅσον ἐκ νηῶν ἀπὸ πύργου τάφρος ἔεργεν, / πλῆθεν ὁμῶς ἵππων τε καὶ ἀνδρῶν ἀσπιστάων, / εἰλομένων 'the whole area away from the ships between the ditch and the wall was filled with chariots and shield-bearing men penned in', i.e., as Ameis also explains, 'the whole space outside the camp enclosed by the ditch away from the wall', i.e. the space between wall and ditch, was filled with fleeing chariots and men. But to form for ourselves a vivid picture of the frenzied flight, particularly at this place into which everyone was crowding tightly together after safely getting over the ditch, we should not imagine too narrow a space. Cf. Hentze, *Appendix*.

In Ι 87 the Greek guards camp at night in the space between wall and ditch: κὰδ δὲ μέσον τάφρου καὶ τείχεος ἷζον ἰόντες· / ἔνθα δὲ πῦρ κήαντο, τίθεντο δὲ δόρπα ἕκαστος 'they took their posts midway between the ditch and the wall, where each lit a fire and laid out food', cf. I 67.

In Σ 215 it is said of Achilles that after receiving the news of Patroclus' death στῆ δ' ἐπὶ τάφρον ἰὼν ἀπὸ τείχεος 'he went and stood at the ditch away from the wall'. A space is also presupposed by Y 49, which is mostly identical with I 67, where it says of Athene αὖε δ' Ἀθήνη / στᾶσ' ὁτὲ μὲν παρὰ τάφρον ὀρυκτὴν *τείχεος ἐκτός* / ἄλλοτ' ἐπ' ἀκτάων ἐριδούπων μακρὸν ἀΰτει 'and Athene raised her war-cry, standing now by the ditch *outside the wall*, and now sending her voice down the thundering shore'.

In the defence of the camp, the ditch plays a part merely as an obstacle; it has to defend itself, so to speak, and during the assault in which the camp is taken by force, it is abandoned without a fight. So it had to be wide so that one could not jump over it, and deep, so that one could not easily get through it, M 53-4 οὔτ' ἄρ' ὑπεκθορέειν σχεδὸν οὔτε περῆσαι ῥηιδίη 'it was not easy to leap over or cross'. But, at the same time, it still had to be passable in at least one place for chariots and infantry which were moving out onto the plain for battle. There is nowhere even a hint of a bridge, however simple and natural such a contrivance appears to us, but there certainly is repeated mention of driving through the ditch. First of all, Λ 47ff. and M 76-7, passages already discussed in my earlier work (pp. 36-7), should be considered. In the former, the Greek advance to battle is described, and we are told that the chariot fighters ordered their drivers to stop the horses at the side of the ditch, 48, that they undertook the marshalling of the army on foot, 49, and that the chariots followed on afterwards. So they had the chariots driving empty from the edge of the ditch – the near one, of course, on the side of the camp – to the marshalling place. The reason for this is quite obvious and can also be deduced from the following passages: in M 76ff. Polydamas advises the Trojans who are advancing victoriously to have the chariots stop at the edge of the ditch, ἐρυκόντων ἐπὶ τάφρῳ 'let them hold the horses at the ditch', as in Λ 48, and to follow Hector across it on foot. His reason for the proposal is that it is difficult enough as it is to drive through the ditch with the chariot, 62 ἀφραδέως διὰ τάφρον ἐλαύνομεν ὠκέας ἵππους, ἡ δὲ μάλ' ἀργαλέη περάαν 'it is folly for us to drive our chariots through the ditch. It is very difficult to cross', but that such a crossing could become absolutely disastrous for the Trojan army if their attack was beaten off and the ditch had to be crossed by chariots and infantry in wild flight, 73 οὐκέτ' ἔπειτ' ὀίω οὐδ' ἄγγελον ἀπονέεσθαι / ἄψορρον προτὶ ἄστυ 'I don't think a single man would escape to bring the news back to the city'. So from this follows – what indeed appears as a quite natural requirement – that the ditch could be crossed carefully and slowly even by chariots, M 58 ἔνθ᾽ οὔ κεν ῥέα ἵππος **[II.6]** ἐΰτροχον ἅρμα τιταίνων / ἐσβαίη 'where horses pulling a chariot could not easily *get through*'. So in one place the sides had been made less steep, but even here the difficulty had not been removed completely in order to keep some degree of protection. That they made the ditch passable only in one or a very few places is a fact which the poet simply assumes in his descriptions, and which seems practical and natural in a camp which was open towards the sea, but only had to be left in the landwards direction when the army was moving out to battle. The assumption of several crossing-places of the ditch is closely connected with the assumption of several gates in the wall – opposite every gate, naturally, you need a crossing-place. Asius, who did not leave his chariot, chose a different place to cross from Hector and the other princes; he leads his men in the assault, 118, νηῶν ἐπ᾽ ἀριστερά, τῇ περ Ἀχαιοὶ / ἐκ πεδίου νίσσοντο σὺν ἵπποισιν καὶ ὄχεσφι· / τῇ ῥ᾽ ἵππους καὶ ἅρμα διήλασεν 'to the left of the ships, where the Greeks had a crossing that they used when returning from the plain with their chariots; there he *drove* his chariot *across*'. It should not surprise us that in most other passages of the *Iliad* only one gate and one crossing-place are assumed, cf. Hentze on M 118. It is well known that similar inconsistencies are found often enough. Diomedes and other Greek leaders also drive through the ditch, Θ 253ff., when they advance to battle again, ἔνθ᾽ οὔ τις πρότερος Δαναῶν, ... εὔξατο Τυδεΐδαο πάρος σχέμεν ὠκέας ἵππους / τάφρου τ᾽ ἐξελάσαι 'Then not one of the Greeks ... could claim he had held his swift horses in front of the son of Tydeus and driven out before him from the ditch'.

Of the flight of the Greeks reported in Θ 335ff. it is stated in quite general terms: οἱ δὲ φέβοντο. / αὐτὰρ ἐπεὶ διά τε σκόλοπας καὶ τάφρον ἔβησαν φεύγοντες κ.τ.λ. 'They turned in panic. But when they had run through the line of the stakes and across the ditch in flight ....' The expression διά τε σκόλοπας 'through the line of stakes' can perhaps be explained by assuming a gap in the row of palisades at the crossing-place. The σκόλοπες 'stakes', put up in a dense row at the edge of the ditch, M 55 ὕπερθεν δὲ σκολόπεσσιν / ὀξέσιν ἤρηρει, τοὺς ἔστασαν υἷες Ἀχαιῶν / πυκνοὺς καὶ μεγάλους δηΐων ἀνδρῶν ἀλεωρήν 'on top there was a row of pointed stakes, close-set and strong, which the Greek troops had planted there to keep out their enemies', constitute a main defence of the ditch. In addition to its depth and breadth, the stakes gave it another security dimension, which made it seem acceptable to dig it some distance away from the wall and not have to locate it under its immediate protection. The crossing of the ditch always remained difficult, as much for an army which had been beaten back to the camp by an assault as for pursuing the enemy beyond the ditch. Therefore in O 1ff., when Poseidon's intervention has reversed the

Trojan success in storming the camp and driven them back in hasty flight, they halted again beyond the ditch only after surmounting these obstacles to flight, αὐτὰρ ἐπεὶ διά τε σκόλοπας καὶ τάφρον ἔβησαν / φεύγοντες, πολλοὶ δὲ δάμεν Δαναῶν ὑπὸ χερσίν, / οἱ μὲν δὴ παρ' ὄχεσφιν ἐρητύοντο μένοντες 'The fleeing Trojans re-crossed the stakes and ditch, many falling at the hands of the Greeks, and did not stop till they reached their chariots'. But with this we are already coming to speak of the significance of the ditch in battle itself, which we had better discuss during our description of the attack on the camp; here we must add something more about security duty in the camp.

Following a pattern favoured by the poet, the establishment of these arrangements appears first as a proposal put in the mouth of the old and militarily experienced Nestor – not as a new and unfamiliar procedure, but as one merely necessary because of nightfall, on the same level as the preparation of the evening meal. It is first mentioned in I 65. The old Pylian interrupts his own speech with the words: ἀλλ' ἦ τοι νῦν μὲν πειθώμεθα νυκτὶ μελαίνη / δόρπα τ' ἐφοπλισσόμεσθα· φυλακτῆρες δὲ ἕκαστοι / λεξάσθων παρὰ τάφρον ὀρυκτὴν τείχεος ἐκτός· / κούροισιν μὲν ταῦτ' ἐπιτέλλομαι 'For the moment, we must take the night into account and eat. Sentries must be posted at intervals along the ditch outside the wall. That is a duty I leave to younger men.'

So because it is evening the young men take up their positions as guards, and are stationed by the ditch outside the wall to prevent a surprise attack or perhaps the preliminaries for an attack like filling in the ditch or creating a crossing point. For, as we saw, the ditch was not an absolute obstacle, but could be crossed and was not under the immediate protection of the wall. The execution of the general order is described at I 80 and shows us, even if one should not over-emphasise the number chosen by the poet **[II.7]**, the great importance which the Greeks attach to security. For seven leaders with 100 men each move to the guard-posts, a disproportionately large number that is probably supposed simply to give special expression to the concern the Greeks feel after their defeat and to show a special caution. The guards then light their fires between the wall and ditch, 87, and cook their meal in the open air. We have to imagine the seven posts as distributed along the front of the camp. The weakest point, the main crossing over the ditch, seems specially secured by a double guard, led furthermore by the two most capable leaders, Meriones and Thrasymedes.

Just as today in a difficult situation the commanding officer satisfies himself of the vigilance of his outposts on whom so much depends, so Agamemnon himself inspects the guards with Nestor, Κ 97ff.: δεῦρ' ἐς τοὺς φύλακας καταβείομεν, ὄφρα ἴδωμεν, / μὴ τοὶ μὲν καμάτῳ ἀδηκότες ἠδὲ καὶ ὕπνῳ / κοιμήσωνται, ἀτὰρ φυλακῆς ἐπὶ πάγχυ λάθωνται 'come

with me and visit the sentries, to make sure they haven't fallen asleep
from exhaustion and lack of sleep, forgetting all about their duties'.
For the enemy are near, 100, and no one knows whether it might not
occur to them to launch an attack at night, 101. But if the situation is
so serious, then all the leaders of the army ought to be vigilant, and
that is why Nestor proposes to Agamemnon, 108, to wake the others
as well. This happens, and the leaders first assemble in front of the
gates by the outposts, 125-6, in order then to move on into the area in
front for an on-the-spot council of war about the current situation.
Everything is found in order among the guards. Their leaders are not
sleeping, nor have they made themselves comfortable by putting down
their weapons, but σὺν τεύχεσιν εἴατο πάντες 182 'they were all sitting
there with their weapons'; their faces were turned steadfastly towards
the enemy, πεδίονδε γὰρ αἰεὶ τετράφαθ᾽ 'all their attention was turned
towards the plain'; they listen attentively to see if they can hear anything from the direction of the Trojans, 189. Nestor therefore rightly
praises them and asks them to continue with equal vigilance. The
leaders themselves then cross the ditch and, quite naturally, invite
the commanders of the two most important outposts, Meriones and
Thrasymedes, to join in their discussion 196-7. Besides, these were
the most immediately available as they were standing with their
guards in the place most at risk, at the usual crossing place over the
ditch – since this is presumably where Nestor and the princes were
just crossing. Now, again at Nestor's suggestion, the council of war
makes a decision which is certainly appropriate to the state of affairs
and which we can unhesitatingly count as among the usual precau-
tions. In order to discover the enemy's intentions, volunteers are sent
over to the Trojans as scouts, 204-5, with orders to capture any of the
enemy who may be hanging around outside the camp, 206, or to find
out in some other way something about the enemy's plans; and indeed
the alternatives that are essentially facing the Trojans are set out
very correctly in 208-9. One could transfer the whole description
directly to a modern setting, only the Homeric volunteer scouts are
rewarded more generously than tends to be the case in our time, for
apart from the honour, κλέος εἴη πάντας ἐπ᾽ ἀνθρώπους 'his fame would
spread world-wide', they are also promised a whole flock of sheep,
213-16. In line with the aim of getting as close to the enemy as possible without making a noise, the scouts are equipped with light helmets which do not gleam or rattle, 255. This precaution is so natural
that we can again take it to be standard practice, even though the
poet describes it to us only once – all the more so as the same sort of
equipment is also mentioned in relation to the scout sent out by
Hector, K 334-5. Dolon too, the Trojan scout, is promised splendid
rewards, since the task of a scout is dangerous; if he was captured it

would be all up with him, and he would be shown no mercy.

[II.8] But in another respect the poet seems to me to make a notable distinction here between the Greeks and the Trojans, as we already observed him do in the advance into battle (p. 51). Apart from the fact that it is reported in K 13, probably quite deliberately, that plenty of things are going on by the Trojans' campfires, (Agamemnon in his tent hears αὐλῶν συρίγγων τ᾽ ἐνοπὴν ὅμαδόν τ᾽ ἀνθρώπων 'the music of their various reed-pipes and the voices of their troops'), the poet does not make them take any measures to protect the troops asleep in the open air. They just fetch food and drink from the city, and with a proud self-confidence lie all night round their numerous fires Θ 553. Certainly this insouciance is supposed to depict vividly the proud, high spirits which animate the Trojans after the victory they have won, but the fact that they abandon themselves to it without thought powerfully illustrates the lack of military competence in barbarians, which is then of course bloodily punished by Diomedes and Odysseus. The fact that the Trojans do not barricade themselves behind a wall and ditch is, of course, caused by the circumstances, and does not indicate the sort of difference that existed for a long time between the Romans sleeping in fortified camps and the barbarians whom they fought; but it is still marked as carelessness that they have not put out any guards. Odysseus expressly asks the captive Dolon about it, 'What about the Trojans' guards and where do they sleep?' K 408, and Dolon answers him with noticeable emphasis on the word φυλακάς 'guards' – there are no special guards protecting the army, 416-17; men designated to stand guard do so only by the Trojans' camp-fires, whereas the allies provide no guards at all. Since this answer still did not exclude the possibility that the allies were camped round the fires together with the Trojans and thus were still enjoying some protection, Odysseus asks a second time whether the allies were camped out separately, and learns that each of their tribes had a camp-site of its own, and that the Thracians in particular, being ἔσχατοι ἄλλων and νεήλυδες 'furthest from the rest' and 'newly arrived', with their king's magnificent horses, would make a night attack worth while. In fact they are sleeping, 471, καμάτῳ ἀδηκότες 'tired out', and have to pay for this carelessness with the loss of numerous fighting men.

That the Greeks, on the other hand, as well trained soldiers, guard their camp even in less dangerous situations than that presented to us in I and K, and carefully set up guard-posts in the manner described just now, and that this security provision already belonged in early times to the natural practices of a Greek camp, can be deduced from the passing mention of it in the description of Priam's journey in Ω. It says there, Ω 443ff.: When they, Hermes and Priam, came to the wall and the ditch (*hysteron proteron*), the guards were busy with the preparation of the evening meal. Ameis incorrectly comments on these passages: 'φυλακτῆρες "guards", who are to be imagined on the inner side of the wall by the locked (446) gate.' It is rather our old friends, the outposts, who are stationed between ditch and wall and therefore in front of the gate and cooking in the open air, naturally again at the very position between the ditch crossing and the main gate, for Priam came by chariot and must have chosen this place to drive in. Then, after Hermes has put the guards to sleep, he opens the gate, 446, which leads into the camp, lets the Trojan king inside the wall with his horses and chariot, and then, once inside the camp, has to slide back the enormous bolt on Achilles' entrance-gate.

[II.9] Attack on and Defence of a Fortified Camp

The camp built by the Greeks is supposed to provide the army with the required accommodation for the duration of the siege, but also with the necessary protection against enemy attacks. For the task of the besieged consists not so much in the actual defence of their walls as in making it impossible for the besieging enemy to remain in front of the city. It is above all the destruction of the enemy's protective and defensive structures which serves to achieve this purpose.

We shall now therefore deal in some more detail with the attack on and defence of a field fortification, to the description of which the poet has devoted a great deal of space. Such encounters necessarily belong to a complete description of the battles of that time, and without them an essential link would be missing in the series of types of battle in Homeric times. Attack on and defence of a fortified camp are positively to be distinguished from the attack on and defence of a fortified city and therefore have to be dealt with in a separate section. This will include a number of additions to the content of the previous chapter on the fortification of the camp, which appear now in the interest of consistency of presentation.

So let us take ourselves into the headquarters of the attacking party to participate along with them in the preparation and execution of the attack. It is true that Hector, Θ 177ff., elated by high-spirited confidence in victory, and in order to inspire the Trojans with equal confidence, understates the difficulties of the military task in hand rather too much when he says of the Greek wall (in recognisable contrast to the city walls): νήπιοι, οἳ ἄρα δὴ τάδε τείχεα μηχανόωντο / ἀβλήχρ᾽, οὐδενόσωρα. τὰ δ᾽ οὐ μένος ἁμὸν ἐρύξει. / ἵπποι δὲ ῥέα τάφρον ὑπερθορέονται ὀρυκτήν 'fools that they are, to have made these flimsy, futile walls, which will not resist my onslaught. As for the ditch they have dug, the horses will jump that with ease'. On the other hand, it appears significant that the Greeks themselves fear the possibility of a successful attack on their camp, I 230ff., whereas the far weaker Trojans show no anxiety about a real attack on the city. Achilles too says clearly, I 351ff., that without him the wall and ditch would not defy a serious assault, whereas earlier, ὄφρα δ' ἐγὼ μετ' Ἀχαιοῖσιν πολέμιζον 'in the days when I took the field with the Greeks', the Trojans would not have dared to fight other than from under the protection of their walls – he does not say behind their walls. So the camp wall is not regarded as offering absolute protection like the walls of the city.

We have to distinguish two types of attack. The first is described to us in Book XII. Hector has led the victorious Trojans right up to the ditch at which the previous day he had had to halt because of nightfall, but which today he hopes to cross, in order to annihilate the Greeks completely if he can. However, the horses of the chariots of the following leaders pull up at the side of the ditch M 50ff., since, as we have seen, the ditch was not easy, 54, to drive through. So they had to dismount and cross the ditch on foot, as the Greeks normally did when they set out for battle, and they could then mount the chariots again on the other side and drive up to the wall. Nothing is said about an attempt by the Greeks to prevent the crossing itself. Also it seems to be naturally assumed that the ditch does not lie under the protection of the wall, and is not defended from it by stone or spear throw. Rather, it must be some way away; otherwise, why would the chariots have had to cross it at all?

[II.10] But Polydamas M 62ff. advises the leaders to do without the small convenience of the chariot drive from the ditch to the wall by also quite correctly considering what would happen if the attack failed, and the best possible way of safeguarding a retreat. Under these circumstances, he says, there would be jostling chaos at the ditch, the chariots in particular would obstruct the crossing, and escape would become impossible. The chariots therefore remain back at the ditch during the assault on the camp; and the army is divided into five groups which form five separate columns each with its own leaders, M 86 διαστάντες σφέας αὐτοὺς ἀρτύναντες 'setting themselves in order in separate groups', and, in close formation, they prepare to begin the attack on the wall, M 105 ἀλλήλους ἄραρον τυκτῇσι βόεσσι 'their oxhide shields touched'. This number of five, however, is completely ignored in the description of the assault itself,[3] and is indeed of no importance at all for our enquiry (Hentze Intr. to M, p. 110, N *App.*, p. 22 at the end). However, the idea is kept in mind that each column chooses a particular point of the wall to assault, so that the camp is attacked at different places simultaneously. The gates naturally constitute the most appropriate point for an attack, and the poet clearly has in mind the image of a camp with several gates; and during the lively and graphic description of the assault which now follows, leading us now to this, now to that point of the furious engagement, this picture is preserved. With a loud battle cry, as during an attack in open field, the men follow their leaders, M 125. Asius, whom we are going to follow to start with, had not left his chariot behind, and leads his company against a gate which had been left open to admit any possible stragglers, in the hope of being able to force his way in more easily there, 126. But the open gate, a particularly weak point, is defended by heroes who are all the braver, who stand outside as steadfast, formidable guards, like Hagen and Volker in front of the lodging in the land of the Huns[4] – 131 τὼ μὲν ἄρα προπάροιθε πυλάων ὑψηλάων / ἕστασαν 'this pair had planted themselves in front of the high gate' – and at the narrow entrance help to repel all attempts at assault. The attackers hold their shields above their heads and with a loud battle cry run at the wall, 137-8: οἱ δ' ἰθὺς πρὸς τεῖχος ἐΰδμητον βόας αὔας / ὑψόσ' ἀνασχόμενοι ἔκιον μεγάλῳ ἀλαλητῷ 'they held up their leather shields and with a mighty shout made straight for the wall'.

The Greeks wait for them to approach and, when they are close to the wall, the two heroes leap forward to prevent their entrance outside the gates, 145 ἐκ δὲ τὼ ἀΐξαντε πυλάων πρόσθε μαχέσθην 'they charged out and fought in front of the gate'. In this they are supported effectively by the other Greeks, who climb the wall and hurl down stones from above, thick as hail, onto the raised shields and helmets of the attackers, stones which had presumably been piled up previously on the wall for this purpose,[5] 154 χερμαδίοισιν ἐϋδμήτων ἀπὸ πύργων / βάλλον 'they flung down stones from the well-built ramparts', 160 κόρυθες δ' ἀμφ' αὖον ἀΰτευν / βαλλόμεναι μυλάκεσσι καὶ ἀσπίδες ὀμφαλόεσσαι 'helmets and bossed shields rang out harshly as the great boulders hit them'. The attacking Trojans also hurl their missiles and hit the defenders, but their hope of success is not fulfilled.

This passage incidentally teaches us what all the others confirm, that the πύργοι 'towers' serve primarily for the protection of the gates, but that they were not particularly high as the men occupying them could be reached by the missiles of the attackers from below.

Another assault force directs its attack immediately against the wall, and tries to force entry through a breach made by force, 256 βίηφι / ῥήγνυσθαι μέγα τεῖχος Ἀχαιῶν πειρήτιζον 'they made determined efforts to breach the great Greek wall'. For this type of attack too it is assumed that the πύργοι 'towers' are not very high, since it is said of the assault force 258: κρόσσας μὲν πύργων ἔρυον καὶ ἔρειπον ἐπάλξεις 'they tore away the parapets of the towers and pulled down the battlements'. They try to tear out by force the buttresses and supports which held together the wall and hope to break through it, while the defenders, using their shields above as a breastwork, try to prevent the attempts at destruction by throwing missiles, 263, ῥινοῖσι βοῶν φράξαντες ἐπάλξεις / βάλλον ἀπ' αὐτάων δηΐους ὑπὸ τεῖχος ἰόντας 'They closed up gaps in the battlements with their oxhide shields and from there threw at the enemy as they came beneath the wall'.

The Greek leaders who, like the attackers, have had sections of the wall allocated to them for defence, **[II.11]** hurry now here, now there, to spur on their men to resist bravely, 265 ἐπὶ πύργων / πάντοσε φοιτήτην 'they ranged everywhere along the walls', and do not tolerate anyone standing around idle. The stones fly like snowflakes from both sides and find their marks, 287 ὡς τῶν ἀμφοτέρωσε λίθοι πωτῶντο θαμειαί, / αἱ μὲν ἄρ' ἐς Τρῶας, αἱ δ' ἐκ Τρώων ἐς Ἀχαιοὺς / βαλλομένων 'so the stones flew thick and fast in both directions as the Greeks pelted the Trojans and the Trojans the Greeks', as the attackers naturally throw back the stones which have been hurled down, as well as their own spears.

The aim of the attack is repeatedly stated to be to force an entry into the camp, whether through a breach, as in the passage discussed above, or by one of the gates. Climbing over the wall is not considered at all; nowhere are ladders or similar aids mentioned. So the attacks are directed above all at the gates and the πύργοι 'towers' which protect them, and therefore, in the general description of the assault, M 35ff., which precedes the presentation of individual actions, the overall impression which we as spectators of the violent conflict get is rightly summed up in the words: τότε δ' ἀμφὶ μάχη ἐνοπή τε δεδήειν / τεῖχος ἐΰδμητον, κανάχιζε δὲ δούρατα πύργων βαλλόμεν' 'the hue and cry of battle flared up round the well built wall, *the woodwork of its towers reverberating* to the enemy's missiles'. The δούρατα πύργων 'woodwork of the towers' should primarily be taken to mean the timber of the gates inserted into the πύργοι 'towers', as is said more clearly in a similarly summary way M 338ff.: ἀϋτὴ δ' οὐρανὸν ἷκε / βαλλομένων σακέων τε καὶ ἱπποκόμων τρυφαλειῶν / καὶ πυλέων, πᾶσαι γὰρ ἐπώχατο, τοὶ δὲ (the Trojans) κατ' αὐτὰς / ἱστάμενοι πειρῶντο βίῃ ῥήξαντες ἐσελθεῖν 'the sky was assaulted by the din as shields, crested helmets, and gates were struck again and again (the gates had all been closed by now and the Trojans were crowding round trying to break them down and force their way in).' But at first the Trojans' attempts remain unsuccessful, in spite of the bravery which the leaders of the individual assault forces display. Amongst them, Sarpedon above all distinguishes himself, and it is his daring which informs us of a further development in the battle for the wall which, like the battle in open field, passes before us in separate pictures. For it must be regarded as a special proof of Sarpedon's courage when he decides to tear down the protecting battlement from the wall with a bold leap, M

308 τεῖχος ἐπαΐξαι διά τε ῥήξασθαι ἐπάλξεις 'to assault the wall and break through the battlements'. If he is successful with the operation, he will of course make the defence of the wall much more difficult, but that it should be regarded as a very special deed of daring is especially imprinted on our minds by the poet through the preceding simile 299-306 of the starving lion who, in spite of dogs and spears, takes an enormous leap into the flock, and through the speech to Glaucus 310-28. Sarpedon, at the head of his Lycians, attacks the πύργος 'tower' defended by Menestheus. The impending danger is recognised by the Achaeans, and a concerned Menestheus looks round for help. Because of the din of battle which has flared up round all the gates, 338-41, he can no longer make himself heard by shouting and sends his aide-de-camp, the κῆρυξ Θοώτης 'herald Thoötes', to get help. At the news of the impending danger, the defending forces gather as quickly as possible at the threatened point, in the same way that troops mass to repel an advance in the field battle (p. 64). Ajax and Teucer also hurry over, naturally τείχεος ἐντὸς ἰόντες 'going along behind the wall' 374, to help drive off the enemy attack and then return to their former position, 369, which at the moment does not seem threatened. In the meantime the Lycians have come up very close, and a loud battle cry accompanies the assault charge and the general man-to-man clash in battle, 377 σὺν δ᾽ ἐβάλοντο μάχεσθαι ἐναντίον, ὦρτο δ᾽ ἀϋτή 'they hurled themselves at the enemy, and the tumult of battle rose'.

During this individual Trojans try to mount the wall, and Ajax shatters Epicles' skull with one of the stones piled up next to the battlements, so that he, 385, ἀρνευτῆρι ἐοικὼς / κάππεσ᾽ ἀφ᾽ ὑψηλοῦ πύργου 'dropped like a diver from the high tower'. Glaucus also is seriously wounded when he tries to climb the wall, ἐπεσσύμενον ... τείχεος ὑψηλοῖο 'as he charged at the high wall' and has to jump down again and leave the battle, 390 ἂψ δ᾽ ἀπὸ τείχεος ἆλτο λαθών 'he jumped unobtrusively down from the wall'. Sarpedon thrusts at a defender with his spear from below, 395 δουρὶ τυχήσας νύξ᾽ 'he stabbed with his spear and hit him' and pulls him down off the wall, ὁ δ᾽ ἑσπόμενος πέσε δουρὶ πρηνής 'the man came with the spear, falling headlong from the wall'. Thereupon Sarpedon grabs the breastwork and pulls [II.12] a long stretch of it down, so that the wall is stripped of its protection and the way opens up for many attackers. So the protective covering consisted of an integrated material, probably wickerwork, which, if torn away in one place, immediately brought further lengths away with it. Ajax and Teucer now simultaneously attack their brave opponent; but he retreats only a little from the breastwork, 406, χώρησεν δ᾽ ἄρα τυτθὸν ἐπάλξιος· οὐδ᾽ ὅ γε πάμπαν χάζετ᾽ 'he withdrew a little from the battlement; even so, he did not retreat completely', and calls on his Lycians to press boldly after him since he cannot, of course, clear the way to the ships all by himself, 410-11, ἀργαλέον δέ μοί ἐστι, καὶ ἰφθίμῳ περ ἐόντι, / μούνῳ ῥηξαμένῳ θέσθαι παρὰ νηυσὶ κέλευθον 'strong as I am, I can hardly breach the wall on my own and open up the way to the ships'. After this the Lycians launch a more powerful assault on the enemy, 414 μᾶλλον ἐπέβρισαν 'they attacked in greater force', but the Greeks also mass close together behind the wall, ἐκαρτύναντο φάλαγγας τείχεος ἔντοσθεν 'they reinforced their contingents behind the wall', and so the two parties stand face to face with each other, separated only by the breastwork between them, across which they hit out and stab at each other, using every opening offered by the enemy, even through the shields, 428-9, so that wall and battlements are spattered with blood. But the Trojans could not gain an inch of ground, nor were the Greeks able to push their enemy back from the wall once they had come right up to it, 417-20.

Now where was Sarpedon standing when, after the destruction of the breastwork, he was spurring on his Lycians, 410. And where were they and the Greeks standing during the fighting mentioned just now, which was intended to force a path for the Trojans to the ships, 418? For Sarpedon it seems reasonable enough to imagine him standing on top of the wall where he has just torn down the breastwork. But it is difficult to reconcile this with the expression χώρησεν δ᾽ ἄρα τυτθὸν ἐπάλξιος 'he withdrew a little from the battlement', 406. How is that supposed to be possible, when the breastwork is naturally fixed on the outer edge of the wall? Even less ought we to imagine the massed battle taking place on the wall. It is said of the Achaeans 415 ἐκαρτύναντο φάλαγγας / τείχεος ἔντοσθεν 'they reinforced their contingents behind the wall', but they could not τείχεος ἂψ ὤσασθαι ἐπεὶ τὰ πρῶτα πέλασθεν 'push [the Lycians] back from the wall once they had come right up to it'. The two parties are separated only by the ἐπάλξιες 'battlements' which have been torn down, 424, over and across which they were thrusting away at each other. So there only remains the assumption that Greeks and Trojans were standing on either side of the wall which, because the battlement had been torn down, had become so low that one could reach the enemy over and across it, not only with a lucky thrust but also by conscious aim, 428-9.

We come across a new picture of a victorious attack when we turn to the contingent of the ablest of the Trojan leaders, Hector. Sarpedon's successes have, of course, had a shattering effect on the Greeks and an encouraging one on the Trojans. During the description 442ff., the situation of 288ff. has not by any means been forgotten, as Hentze alleges in his *Appendix*; rather, both deeds, those of Sarpedon and Hector, interact. Hector's troops, of course, have not been watching idly up to now, but have participated in the general bombardment of the wall; now he can lead them forward to assault it,

440-1: ὄρνυσθ' ἱππόδαμοι Τρῶες, ῥήγνυσθε δὲ τεῖχος / Ἀργείων καὶ νηυσὶν ἐνίετε θεσπιδαὲς πῦρ 'On with you, horse-taming Trojans, smash the Greek wall and fire the ships!' They close their ranks for a massed attack, 443, ἴθυσαν δ' ἐπὶ τεῖχος ἀολλέες 'Massing together, they charged at the wall' and while his companions attack the battlements with their spears, κροσσάων ἐπέβαινον ἀκαχμένα δούρατ' ἔχοντες 'they began to scale the parapet with sharp spears in their hands' 444, and try to drive back the defenders and tear down the battlements in order to make Hector's plan easier by forcefully occupying the attention of the enemy. Hector 'heaves up' (imperfect, φέρεν 'proceeded to carry') an enormous stone, goes right up to the gate, 457, and hurls it with gigantic force against it, so that the hinges and bolts collapse, and the stone drops down on the inside of the gate. Hector storms after it swinging his spears, the Greeks retreat in shock, and the Trojans dash after their victorious leader through the gate and over the wall, 469: αὐτίκα δ' οἱ μὲν τεῖχος ὑπέρβασαν, οἱ δὲ κατ' αὐτὰς / ποιητὰς **[II.13]** ἐσέχυντο πύλας 'some swarmed over the wall, others poured in through the gate itself'. Hector himself had called on his men to climb over the wall, 468. Now that the defenders had abandoned it, it no longer posed a substantial obstacle to surmount. This passage too indicates that we should not imagine the wall as being very high. For not only did Hector's companions choose the shortest way over the wall, but we have also to imagine the victors now swiftly taking this route into the enemy camp everywhere else, as Poseidon says expressly at N 50 (cf. 87): Τρώων, οἳ μέγα τεῖχος ὑπερκατέβησαν ὁμίλῳ 'the Trojans who have climbed over the great wall in force'. But the actual breakthrough had been brought about by the smashing of the gate, the deed of the bravest hero, Hector.

Asius also appears among the fighting Trojans N 385 with his chariot. Even if I accept certain inconsistencies in Book XIII, I cannot with Ribbeck (cf. Ameis *App.* ad loc.)[6] find any difficulty in this. Nor is it necessary with Hentze to assume that breaches have been made in the wall for the Trojans' advance. The most natural explanation is surely that, in the general Greek retreat, Asius had forced his way in through the gate which had been first attacked by him and so bravely defended until now. A specific statement that this has happened is not necessary. The poet describes the whole battle for the wall for us by proceeding group by group in such a way that the actual breakthrough is credited to Hector, and the other groups mentioned are afterwards disregarded. Fully in accordance with the idea that the Trojans advanced along the whole line, over the wall or through the gates, the battle naturally then continues inside the Greek camp. Hector is still to be found near the gate, N 679, ᾗ τὰ πρῶτα πύλας καὶ τεῖχος ἐσᾶλτο 'where he had first stormed the gate and wall'. But I do not refer the words of the following verse ῥηξάμενος Δαναῶν πυκινὰς στίχας ἀσπιστάων 'breaking the shield-bearing ranks of the Greeks' to the battle on the plain, as Düntzer does ('this refers to the defeat on the plain after which they fled behind the ditch and wall'), but to the bloody battle for the wall; and I find the expression ῥηξάμενος στίχας 'breaking the ranks', which is particularly characteristic of success won in battle (cf. p. 63), especially appropriate in our passage, where the Greek withdrawal from a long-held defensive position is to be described.

The wall itself looked in a bad way after the assault. Even if it had not been destroyed completely, the attacking Trojans had still achieved their aim, M 258 κρόσσας μὲν πύργων ἔρυον καὶ ἔρειπον ἐπάλξεις 'they tore away the parapets of the towers, and pulled down the battlements', and had generally torn down the protective breastworks. However, they could not hold their own in the Greek camp and, when Poseidon intervened effectively on behalf of the Greeks, they had to give up all their gains and go back over the wall and ditch onto the plain again. Only Zeus' awakening restores their fortunes in battle, and in Book XV, which in general contains particularly clearly described battle scenes, the poet presents us with a second assault on the fortified camp. Here we experience a new kind of attack, which develops clearly and vividly before our eyes.

To safeguard the retreat of the multitude of Achaeans who are fleeing in panic back from the plain, on old Thoas' advice, O 281, a group of important Greek leaders with their men, 300ff., had taken up a defensive position and tried to delay the victorious Trojan advance long enough for the great mass of Greeks to reach the ships, 295. This undertaking, which is in itself to be applauded as a brave and determined action, implemented at the right time, gains even more importance when we consider how difficult it must have been to shepherd an army in flight across the ditch, immediately in front of the pursuing enemy.

Apollo leads the Trojan army to attack the defensive formation of the Greeks, O 307. After a brief resistance, during which many missiles are hurled on both sides and **[II.14]** many warriors are wounded, 319, the Greek line is broken, 328, and they turn towards the ditch, 326, in hurried flight, following the bulk of the army. The Trojans pursue them and try to do as much damage as they can to the routed enemy, 328-42. In accordance with Homeric battle description, it is only Greeks in flight who meet their death at this time. The remainder rush to the ditch and the palisades which protect it, 344 τάφρῳ καὶ σκολόπεσσιν ἐνιπλήξαντες ὀρυκτῇ 'forced into the ditch and palisade'. I like to see it as no coincidence that, for the Greeks who are arriving from the outside, the ditch is mentioned first and the palisades which stand on the inner margin second, whereas at O 1 it is put the other way round for the Trojans fleeing from the camp to the city: αὐτὰρ ἐπεὶ διά τε σκόλοπας καὶ τάφρον ἔβησαν 'but when they had crossed the palisade and ditch'. After the ditch has been crossed, the men flee in all directions, ἔνθα καὶ ἔνθα φέβοντο 'dashed in panic this way and that' 345. So after crossing the small causeway across the ditch, which had kept the fleeing masses together, they dispersed right and left in order to get behind the safe protection of the palisades and the wall as quickly as possible. But Hector keeps firmly in mind the main goal, the destruction of the enemy. Whilst threatening with violence those who are lagging behind to get booty, O 347, he concentrates all his troops for a general advance. Individual assault forces are not detailed off first, nor is the fortification attacked at different places, but there is a general advance accompanied by a loud battle cry, 355, which has as its goal a direct attack on the wall over the ditch, all along the line.

That such a procedure for an assault all along the line of the wall is put in place at a time when the enemy, still demoralised from the defeat they have just suffered, cannot summon up any real energy to resist, is a touch based on the subtle observation of reality by our militarily experienced poet.

But in order to be able to cross the ditch in an assault by the whole army, the way has to be prepared and the crossing-place considerably widened. This is why Apollo goes in front of the assault column, as sappers did in later times or, among the Romans, individual soldiers expressly given this task, and smoothes the way for the assault troops, 356, ῥεῖ' ὄχθας καπέτοιο βαθείης ποσσὶν ἐρείπων / ἐς μέσσον κατέβαλλε, γεφύρωσεν δὲ κέλευθον / μακρὴν ἠδ' εὐρεῖαν 'he easily kicked in the sides of the deep ditch and piled them into the middle, making a broad and ample causeway'. And when they have crossed the ditch φαλαγγηδόν 'rank after rank', he continues to hurry ahead and also makes a breach in the wall in front of them, 360, τῇ ῥ' οἵ γε προχέοντο φαλαγγηδόν, πρὸ δ' Ἀπόλλων / αἰγίδ' ἔχων ἐρίτιμον· ἔρειπε δὲ τεῖχος Ἀχαιῶν / ῥεῖα μάλ' 'Here they poured across rank after rank, led by Apollo, holding up the precious aegis. Then, with equal ease, the god knocked down the Greek wall', and the victorious Trojans pour through after him into the Greek camp, even with their chariots, 384ff.

It is obvious that this general attack was significantly facilitated by the extensive damage to the wall during the first assault. But Homer's poetic description does not treat this as an absolute prerequisite, and nowhere is it mentioned even by way of a hint. It is simply a completely new type of attack which is described to us here, which can equally easily be viewed quite independently as the first attack on an enemy field fortification. I have spoken elsewhere (p. 38) of the description of the desperate battle which now arises by the ships, and I added there that in the narrative of the battle itself the chariots, whose mention during the assault, 385, made the Trojans' success seem even greater, are immediately forgotten.

If during the rout of the Trojans which occurs later the crossing of the ditch proves difficult again and considerably hampers the speed of flight, Π 369ff. οὓς (sc. Τρῶας) ἀέκοντας ὀρυκτὴ τάφρος ἔρυκεν. / πολλοὶ δ᾽ ἐν τάφρῳ ἐρυσάρματες ὠκέες ἵπποι / ἄξαντ᾽ ἐν πρώτῳ ῥυμῷ λίπον ἅρματ᾽ ἀνάκτων 'who (i.e. the Trojans) were held back by the ditch against their will. For many a pair of swift horses snapped off their shafts at the yoke in the ditch, leaving their masters' chariots behind', one need not conclude from this that the causeway made by Apollo has been forgotten, cf. Ameis ad loc.: 'It is striking that here the causeway **[II.15]** across the ditch created by Apollo is not mentioned'. Rather, the whole description has certainly been taken from real life. During the assault by the whole army, it was not a complete causeway which was built; rather the ditch was partially filled in only as immediately required, and as quickly as possible, by pushing in the sides. This loose rubble is gradually trodden down as the whole army crosses it, and during the flight the ditch can again constitute a considerable obstacle. Besides, Apollo had not made the path any wider than fifteen to twenty paces, Ο 358 ὅσον τ᾽ ἐπὶ δουρὸς ἐρωὴ / γίγνεται 'wide as the distance a man throws a spear', a little narrow for an army in wild flight, so that many men might try to cross to one side of it. The real task of the Trojans, completely to destroy the fortified camp of the Greeks after their successful assault, remained unfulfilled because they were once again driven back out of the camp.

We turn now to the discussion of:

Siege and Defence of a Fortified City

At the centre of the events described in the *Iliad* lies the siege of the strong city of Priam, surrounded by walls, whose capture is described as the goal and purpose of the powerful expedition which had mobilised the whole of Greece. But whereas we get vivid, detailed descriptions of all other kinds of conflict, which give us an insight into a well-developed method of fighting involving the use of all available means, we learn virtually nothing about the actual military procedures and measures appropriate for capturing a town under siege by stratagem or force.

Of course, according to the poet's plan all the battles and deeds of valour presented to us take place while the city is under siege, and its capture is not to be described in the *Iliad* at all; but nothing happens either which could bring about an enforced surrender or prepare for a violent assault, or could point to the intention of making any aggressive move against the besieged city with the far superior Greek army.

On the other hand we have repeated reports of the capture of enemy cities: I 328-9 Achilles boasts δώδεκα δὴ σὺν νηυσὶ πόλεις ἀλάπαξ· ἀνθρώπων / πεζὸς δ᾽ ἕνδεκά φημι κατὰ Τροίην ἐρίβωλον 'I have captured twelve towns by sea and eleven by land across fertile Troy', cf. I 666-8; at Α 367 the same hero says ᾠχόμεθ᾽ ἐς Θήβην ... τὴν δὲ διεπράθομεν 'We went to Thebe ... and sacked it', Λ 625 τὴν ('Εκαμήδην) ἄρετ᾽ ἐκ Τενέδοιο γέρων, ὅτε πέρσεν Ἀχιλλεύς 'The old man had won her [Hecamede] when Achilles sacked Tenedos' and Ζ 415ff. Andromache reports the destruction of her home city Thebe by the same prince. In this passage it seems to me a significant fact that Achilles had killed all her brothers, Ζ 423-4, βουσὶν ἐπ᾽ εἰλιπόδεσσι καὶ ἀργεννῇς ὀίεσσιν 'while they were looking after their shambling cattle and white sheep', i.e. not during the defence of the city. Presumably therefore we shall not go wrong if we assume that Thebe and the numerous other cities which had been destroyed and plundered in the region around Troy were either not at all or just weakly fortified, and easily succumbed to the attack of a well-armed raiding force, whereas with Troy we are dealing with the main city of the country, a properly fortified place whose walls offered almost absolute protection against the as yet undeveloped art of siege. The honorific epithet πτολίπορθος 'sacker of cities' which Achilles is sometimes given in the *Iliad*, Θ 372, Ο 77, Φ 550, Ω 108 – Oileus Β 728 and Otrynteus Υ 384 are also so named[7] – therefore refers to the destruction of enemy settlements which brought more in the way of booty than military glory **[II.16]**. All the same, it is to be expected that this often did not happen without fierce fighting, which is expressly reported in relation to the destruction of the town Lyrnessus, of which the weeping Briseis says Τ 291ff: ἄνδρα μέν ... εἶδον πρὸ πτόλιος δεδαϊγμένον ὀξέϊ χαλκῷ / τρεῖς τε κασιγνήτους ... / κηδείους, οἳ πάντες ὀλέθριον ἦμαρ ἐπέσπον 'I saw my husband ... mangled in front of his town by the cruel spear; and I saw my three dear brothers ... all meet their doom'; it is also said of her Β 690ff.: τὴν (Βρισηΐδα) ἐκ Λυρνησσοῦ ἐξείλετο πολλὰ μογήσας, Λυρνησσὸν διαπορθήσας καὶ τείχεα Θήβης, / κὰδ δὲ Μύνητ᾽ ἔβαλεν καὶ 'Επίστροφον ἐγχεσιμώρους, '[Briseis] whom he had won from Lyrnessus after much hard toil, when he sacked Lyrnessus itself and stormed the walls of Thebe and brought down the spearmen Mynes and Epistrophus'. But the destruction of this city too had taken place on the occasion of a raid, whereas the Greeks lay camped out before Troy for ten years without the massive fortification walls with which the city of Priam is said to be surrounded, and which the original of the poetic description historically possessed, allowing them to advance a single step. All the same, is it not a siege which has in mind eventual capture as its goal and indeed an attainable, possible goal? Certainly the capture of the city had to be possible if the mobilising of such enormous forces is to be conceivable, and without doubt Troy – or whatever else we want to call the strong fortress on the coast of Asia Minor – eventually succumbed to the perseverance of the Greeks or their βουλῇ 'strategy' and was destroyed (cf. χ 230 where it is said of Odysseus: σῇ δ᾽ ἥλω βουλῇ Πριάμου πόλις εὐρυάγυια 'The city of Priam with its broad streets was captured by your plan'); all the same there is not as yet any trace of an art of siege and violent assault.

The poet very frequently gives expression, through the mouths of individual heroes, to the hope that the goal will finally be attained, indeed to the certainty of that imminent fall. I shall discuss only some of the numerous passages of this kind. The wish that Troy will be destroyed is first put in the mouth of the priest Chryses, A 19 ὑμῖν μὲν θεοὶ δοῖεν ... / ἐκπέρσαι Πριάμοιο πόλιν εὖ δ᾽ οἴκαδ᾽ ἱκέσθαι 'May the gods grant you ... to sack Priam's town and get home in safety', and just as generally does Achilles express the thought A 129: αἴ κέ ποθι Ζεὺς / δῶσι πόλιν Τροίην εὐτείχεον ἐξαλαπάξαι 'if Zeus ever grants us to sack the Trojan city with its fine walls'. The epithet εὐτείχεον 'with fine walls' seems worth noting in this expression, particularly because it is included in other passages which contain the same thought. So we read in B 113, 288, Ƌ 716, I 20, cf. Θ 241, that Zeus has promised Agamemnon or Menelaus Ἴλιον ἐκπέρσαντ᾽ εὐτείχεον ἀπονέεσθαι 'to sack Ilium with its fine walls and return home'. Is that not supposed to mean that it is precisely the τείχεα 'walls' of the city which make its destruction difficult, so that Zeus will hand Troy over to the Greeks in spite of the walls? This promise will become impossible to fulfil, Hera adds Ƌ 717, if the gods allow Ares to continue to rage like this on the field of battle. At B 12 (29) Zeus has Agamemnon deceitfully informed by the dream-god that he should get all the Achaeans to arm themselves, νῦν γάρ κεν ἕλοι πόλιν εὐρυάγυιαν / Τρώων 'for the chance of capturing the Trojans' town with its broad streets has now come', because the gods are no longer in disagreement over this question. But the dream-god does not add *how* this could happen, and because of this Agamemnon, who foolishly believes that the dream is true, B 38 φῆ γὰρ ὅ γ᾽ αἱρήσειν Πριάμου πόλιν ἤματι κείνῳ / νήπιος 'he imagined he would capture Priam's town that very day, the fool', does not find much credence in the council of the elders (B 53) with the old and experienced Nestor, by whom his plan is very coolly received, 79ff. From Agamemnon's speech in the assembly of the people we do indeed learn, B 117, that Zeus has already πολλάων πολίων κατέλυσε κάρηνα 'brought down the high towers of many a town', but Agamemnon does not give any information about how this has happened. In fact, the

Greeks' confidence in eventual success seems generally to have been shaken by the long unsuccessful siege, and Odysseus succeeds only with difficulty in bringing back to the assembly the men rushing to the boats, by giving them the assurance, B 329, τῷ δεκάτῳ δὲ πόλιν αἱρήσομεν εὐρυάγυιαν 'In the tenth year Ilium's broad streets will be ours'. Therefore they should stay εἰς ὅ κεν ἄστυ μέγα Πριάμοιο ἕλωμεν 'till we capture Priam's great city' 332. Agamemnon himself also has finally lost heart and I 28 seriously considers giving up the siege without any attempt to capture the city by force, οὐ γὰρ ἔτι Τροίην αἱρήσομεν εὐρυάγυιαν 'The Trojans' town with its broad streets will never fall to us'; but Diomedes wants to stay, 46, εἰς ὅ κέ περ Τροίην διαπέρσομεν 'until we have sacked Troy'. To judge from Nestor's turn of phrase – which is kept a little general and which he adds to his proposal for drawing up the army by contingents B 367 – that with this formation Agamemnon **[II.17]** will discover 'whether a decision by the gods is to blame, not simply the cowardice and inexperience of the warriors, if he does not destroy Troy', we can gather only that the good formation of the army on the field of battle is important also for the eventual capture of the city.

But what steps did the besiegers take, since there is no mention of starving people out, destroying the water supply or other hostile action? According to our ideas, not very much which served the purpose of capture – though that, of course, does make the long duration of a siege all the more understandable. Let us first ask, what instructions does Agamemnon come up with, B 381ff., to realise his hopes, since the poet has made him convinced that he will capture Troy on this very day? He only orders the army to make all the preparations for battle, B 381, ἵνα ξυνάγωμεν Ἄρηα 'so that we may join battle'; he says they will fight all day without a break until nightfall, and no one should think for a moment about keeping out of the fighting. From the whole of the development that follows – the mustering of the army, the advance and the combat – it emerges that the battle which is supposed to lead to the capture of Troy means a field battle on the plain in front of the walls of the besieged city. This one example immediately gives us in essence the complete tactics for the siege and defence of fortified cities in Homeric time. The two armies, besieging and defending, advance against each other, and the decision who will have control of the city in the future is contested in front of its walls. How long this lasts, and how often the die of battle has to be cast, is a question of the relative strengths.

But first let us look for further evidence for this statement.

After Agamemnon has announced to the assembly his plan to offer battle to the Trojans in order to realise his dream, even Nestor shows himself to be in complete agreement, and calls on the Achaeans to proceed to action immediately, B 435 μηδέ τι δηρὸν / ἀμβαλλώμεθα ἔργον, ὃ δὴ θεὸς ἐγγυαλίζει 'and not put off the work that the god has set our hands to' and to do everything, ὄφρα κε θᾶσσον ἐγείρομεν ὀξὺν Ἄρηα 'so that we may the sooner begin battle'. The Achaeans are deployed accordingly B 477 ὑσμίνηνδ' ἰέναι 'to advance to battle' and Iris 801 informs Hector that the Greeks ἔρχονται πεδίοιο μαχησόμενοι προτὶ ἄστυ 'are advancing over the plain to fight at the town', whereupon he leads out the Trojans and likewise draws them up for battle at the hill Batieia, 809ff.

In the same way Achilles describes his task before Troy as ἀμφιμάχεσθαι 'to fight round the city', I 412 εἰ μέν κ' αὖθι μένων Τρώων πόλιν ἀμφιμάχωμαι 'if I stay and here and fight it out round the city of the Trojans', and Hector likewise says of the activity of the two hostile sides, Z 461, that they Ἴλιον ἀμφεμάχοντο 'fought it out round Ilium'. The description Phoenix gives of the Curetes' siege of Calydon, the main city of the Aetolians, is also important for our question. The general description of the siege is given I 529-31 with the words: Κουρῆτές τ' ἐμάχοντο καὶ Αἰτωλοὶ μενεχάρμαι / ἀμφὶ πόλιν Καλυδῶνα καὶ ἀλλήλους ἐνάριζον, / Αἰτωλοὶ μὲν ἀμυνόμενοι ... Κουρῆτες δὲ διαπραθέειν μεμαῶτες Ἄρηϊ 'The Curetes *were fighting* the warlike Aetolians around the town of Calydon, and losses were heavy on both sides. The Aetolians were defending [Calydon] ... and the Curetes doing all they could to sack it'; and, of the Curetes when they were besieged and defending themselves, it is said, to indicate the straits they were in, I 550-2, ὄφρα ... Μελέαγρος ... πολέμιζεν, / τόφρα δὲ Κουρήτεσσι κακῶς ἦν οὐδὲ δύναντο / *τείχεος ἔκτοσθεν μίμνειν* πολέες περ ἐόντες, 'as long as Meleager was in the battle, things went badly for the Curetes who were unable *to hold their ground outside the walls*, for all their numbers'. Meleager, too, who is being besieged in Calydon, is asked in these dire straits, 576, ἐξελθεῖν καὶ ἀμῦναι 'to go out and fight' i.e. to defend his home city outside, in front of the gates. It is a deviation from the usual siege tactics employed against Troy when it is said that Calydon is bombarded (compare what happened during the attack on the Greek camp, above) 587ff. οὐδ' ... ἔπειθον / πρίν γ' ὅτε δὴ θάλαμος πύκ' ἐβάλλετο, τοὶ δ' ἐπὶ πύργων / βαῖνον Κουρῆτες καὶ ἐνέπρηθον μέγα ἄστυ 'Even so they could not ... win him over, until the Curetes began scaling the walls and setting fire to the great town'. Then Meleager at the last moment succeeds in beating back the enemy – it is not reported how – and Αἰτωλοίσιν ἀπήμυνεν κακὸν ἦμαρ 'saved the Aetolians from disaster', I 597.

However, the art of siege is significantly more developed on the **[II.18]** silver bowl from Amathus[8] which Helbig uses to analyse the arrangement of the scenes on the shield of Achilles, cf. Helbig, *Das homerische Epos* (2nd ed.), pp. 39 and 411. There we see towers rising high above the walls, scaling ladders erected and climbed, and fruit trees in the area surrounding the besieged city being cut down. But the *Iliad* does not yet know of scaling ladders or similar aids. It is true that Andromache Z 433ff. asks Hector to draw up his troops inside the wall in the place ἔνθα μάλιστα / ἄμβατός ἐστι πόλις καὶ ἐπίδρομον ἔπλετο τεῖχος 'where the town is most open to attack and the wall easiest to scale' and she reminds him that the best Greek heroes have attempted to force their way in at this place three times already, τῇ γ᾽ ἐλθόντες ἐπειρήσανθ᾽ 'they have come there and tried to force their way in'. But nothing more precise is added about the nature of this attempt, and the addition 438-9 ἤ πού τίς σφιν ἔνισπε θεοπροπίων ἐΰ εἰδώς, / ἤ νυ καὶ αὐτῶν θυμὸς ἐποτρύνει καὶ ἀνώγει 'Someone who knows the oracles must have told them about it or else they have their own reasons for attacking there' allows us to conclude that this was not an actual attack but a surprise strike against the city at a weaker part of the wall. Hector wants to prevent such a strike Θ 521 when, in the absence of the army, he has the walls guarded by boys and old men, φυλακὴ δέ τις ἔμπεδος ἔστω, / μὴ λόχος εἰσέλθῃσι πόλιν λαῶν ἀπεόντων 'regular guards must be mounted so that no enemy raiding-party can steal into the town while the troops are away'. Again, the besieged people on Achilles' shield leave the protection of the wall to their wives, old men and children when they make a sortie, Σ 514-15.

The possibility of scaling the walls is also expressed in other passages; thus Hector says to the fleeing Diomedes Θ 165 οὐκ ... πύργων ἡμετέρων ἐπιβήσεαι, οὐδὲ γυναῖκας / ἄξεις ἐν νήεσσι 'you will not climb our walls or carry off our women in your ships', but the expression πύργων ἐπιβαίνειν 'to climb the walls' should be understood more generally as a symbolic description of victory, 'to set your foot on our wall', as was possible if fortifications were weak. A capture by assault would of course have represented the most magnificent heroic achievement, but its fulfilment did not lie within the scope of ordinary human strength. The poet therefore pays Patroclus' heroic strength the highest honour, when he describes him almost gaining this finest prize of victory, Π 698ff., ἔνθα κεν ὑψίπυλον Τροίην ἕλον υἷες Ἀχαιῶν / Πατρόκλου ὑπὸ χερσί ... τρὶς μὲν ἐπ᾽ ἀγκῶνος βῆ τείχεος ὑψηλοῖο / Πάτροκλος, τρὶς δ᾽ αὐτὸν ἀπεστυφέλιξεν Ἀπόλλων, / χείρεσσ᾽ ... φαεινὴν ἀσπίδα νύσσων 'the Trojans' city with its high gates would now have fallen to the Greeks under Patroclus ... three times Patroclus scaled an angle of the high wall and three times Apollo forced him back, thrusting at his glittering shield with his hands'. So three times – and these were the moments of greatest danger for Troy – Patroclus had stepped on to the ledge of the wall, but three times Apollo, who ἐϋδμήτου ἐπὶ πύργου / ἔστη 'stood on the well-built tower' 700 (we should certainly not think of a tower much higher than the wall), hurls him back, pushing the shield with his hands. It is left to our imagination to speculate how Patroclus would have got up the wall itself. With these words the poet does not intend to describe a way of taking the city by storm; he merely wants to recount a supremely powerful, superhuman feat by his hero. (We can quote as an analogy Sarpedon's feat, M 397ff., when he tears down the battlement of the wall during the assault on the Greek camp.) But, in any case, the whole narrative, 698-711, contradicts the preceding and following verses and has rightly caused offence to numerous commentators. Of the contradictions I shall mention just one, that at 733 Patroclus appears on his chariot and jumps down only for the duel with Hector – which fits in splendidly with the situation described, the pursuit of the Trojans – and that 784ff. are inconsistent with the idea that Patroclus had previously reached the ledge of the wall. Incidentally, it is typical that the Trojans here, in dire straits because of Patroclus, defend their city in front of the gates, Π 712ff., as they did in the *aristeia* of Diomedes, whereas when the Greeks are pursued, they immediately flee behind the protection of their fortifications and try to fend off the pursuing enemy from behind the wall; and that it is not until the greatest climax, their pursuit by Achilles, that the Trojans all withdraw into the city, and are then however completely secure, even from this most dangerous enemy, behind the walls. It is true that, after Hector's death, Achilles, X 381-4 **[II.19]** for a moment plans an attempt against Troy, ἀμφὶ πόλιν σὺν τεύχεσι πειρηθέωμεν / ὄφρα κ' ἔτι γνῶμεν Τρώων νόον ..., ἢ καταλείψουσιν πόλιν ἄκρην τοῦδε πεσόντος, / ἦε μένειν μεμάασι 'let's make a circuit of the town under arms and find out what the Trojans mean to do next, whether they will abandon their citadel now that Hector has fallen, or make up their minds to hold it', but the general expression πειρηθέωμεν ἀμφὶ πόλιν 'let's make a circuit of the town' does not give any information whatsoever about the type of attack which is possibly envisaged. I am not quite sure what one should understand by καταλείψουσιν πόλιν 'they will abandon their town' and the passage is also suspect for other reasons. Cf. Hentze ad loc.

So one can hardly call this waiting around by the Greeks a siege, and it is probably in view of this that Thucydides I 11.2 says πολιορκίᾳ δ' ἂν προσκαθεζόμενοι ἐν ἐλάσσονί τε χρόνῳ καὶ ἀπονώτερον τὴν Τροίαν εἷλον 'if they had stuck to the siege, they would have taken Troy in less time and with less trouble', but the reason for this obviously lies in the fact that, at that time, the art of siege was unknown. The reason offered by Thucydides for the long duration of the siege in the passage mentioned does of course have a certain validity, i.e. that the Greeks never confronted the Trojans at full strength because they had to carry out raids in the surrounding areas in order to maintain the army, εἰ ... ὄντες ἀθρόοι ἄνευ ληστείας καὶ γεωργίας συνεχῶς τὸν πόλεμον διέφερον (had carried on), ῥᾳδίως ἂν μάχῃ κρατοῦντες εἷλον, οἵ γε καὶ οὐκ ἀθρόοι ἀλλὰ μέρει τῷ ἀεὶ παρόντι ἀντεῖχον 'If ... they had kept together and prosecuted the war without raiding and farming, they would easily have defeated the Trojans in the field and taken the city, since they held their own against them when they were not all together but with whatever part of their army was available'; but these raids into the surrounding country were as necessary for feeding the army as *mutatis mutandis* they still are today. For what the Greek historian offers as the condition of a speedier resolution of the war – περιουσίαν δὲ εἰ ἦλθον ἔχοντες τροφῆς 'if they had brought plenty of supplies with them' – was a simple impossibility, even if he was right in his judgement that the Greek army was smaller from the start simply because of the difficulty of providing food: *ibid.* 1 τῆς γὰρ τροφῆς ἀπορίᾳ τόν τε στρατὸν ἐλάσσω ἤγαγον καὶ ὅσον ἤλπιζον αὐτόθεν πολεμοῦντα βιοτεύσειν 'Because of the difficulty of supplying the army, they reduced the troops to a number which they hoped they could sustain from the countryside while they fought the war'. We have discussed above the need to protect the besieging army by means of a fortified camp. This necessity was so absolute that the proposal put in Agamemnon's mouth Ξ 65ff., to sail for home after the Greek camp has been taken by the Trojans, should not by any means be regarded simply as a counsel of despair. Agamemnon's cowardice lies only in the fact that he does not think of rebuilding the destroyed fortifications.

The fate of a captured city, a glimpse of which the poet allows us on several occasions, is fixed from the outset. It will, as a matter of course, be burnt down. Capture and destruction by fire are almost always mentioned together, and the excavations in the countryside of the Troad at the ancient sites of the battles between Greeks and Asiatics have given clear enough confirmation of the truth of this close connection. In B 412 Agamemnon asks Zeus: μὴ πρὶν ἐπ' ἠέλιον δῦναι καὶ ἐπὶ κνέφας ἐλθεῖν / πρίν με κατὰ πρηνὲς βαλέειν Πριάμοιο μέλαθρον / αἰθαλόεν, πρῆσαι δὲ πυρὸς δηΐοιο θύρετρα 'that the sun may not set and darkness fall before I bring Priam's smoke-blackened palace crashing down and send his gates up in flames'. In I 591 we hear from the mouth of Cleopatra, wife of Meleager, what was in store for the besieged: κήδε' ὅσ' ἀνθρώποισι πέλει, τῶν ἄστυ ἁλώῃ· / ἄνδρας μὲν κτείνουσι, πόλιν δέ τε πῦρ ἀμαθύνει, / τέκνα δέ τ' ἄλλοι ἄγουσι βαθυζώνους τε γυναῖκας 'all the miseries people suffer when their town is captured: they kill the men, fire levels the town, the enemy carry off the children and low-girdled women'. In moving words Priam X 61ff. pictures the fate awaiting him in the case of the capture of the city, but the most heart-rending to us is the lament in the mouths of Hector and Andromache Z 407ff. about the cruel, appalling fate that awaits a city that is taken.

The inhabitants of a city naturally did everything in their power to ward off such a fate. Effective fortification offered the best protection, but most of the cities by far fell short of this, as the large number destroyed in the countryside of the Troad proves. But we cannot gain a precise concept of the nature of such fortifications from Homer alone; for this purpose we need to enlist the help provided for us by Schliemann's excavations.[9] The picture of the nature of the fortress once situated on Hissarlik given us by the walls of the first period **[II.20]** ought in general to correspond to the picture of the city around whose fortifications the poet has his heroes fight out their battles. A colossal wall – I draw on the description in Rudolf Menge's *Troia und die Troas* – surrounded the fortress; on Hissarlik its top was 2.70 metres thick. The poet does not give us any information about the material out of which he has had it built. He uses the word τεῖχος for the wall which the Greeks have piled up round their camp, as much as for the fortification wall of the city, and also Υ 145 he speaks of the τεῖχος ... ἀμφίχυτον Ἡρακλῆος θείοιο / ὑψηλόν, τό ῥά οἱ Τρῶες καὶ Παλλὰς Ἀθήνη / ποίεον, ὄφρα τὸ κῆτος ὑπεκπροφυγὼν ἀλέαιτο, / ὁππότε μιν σεύαιτο ἀπ᾽ ἠϊόνος πεδίονδε 'the high wall that the Trojans and Pallas Athene made for godlike Heracles, as a place of refuge for him when the sea-monster came up from the beach to attack him on dry land'.

Nor can the material be identified from the epithets which the poet attaches to the word τεῖχος 'wall', but we shall probably not be mistaken if we assume that the wall of the poetic city of Troy, i.e. of a fortified city at the time of the poet, had been built of air-dried bricks. It was also provided with towers. From the poem itself we cannot glean much about their composition, size or use, either. But when we consider the fact that the πύργοι 'towers' in the walls of the Greek camp were not to be assumed to be higher than the wall itself, but only thicker and wider; and that not a single passage of the *Iliad* indicates that the towers of Troy were higher than the wall, but rather that in very many passages πύργος 'tower' is used virtually synonymously with τεῖχος 'wall', the assumption seems to me very probable that in the fortification of the city too the πύργοι 'towers' were essentially simply reinforcements of the wall, extensions whose purpose was to gather a considerable number of defenders in one place, to prevent possible destructive enemy activity more easily. Presumably they had also built in them steps for defenders to climb the wall as well as for the old, who used to watch the battle raging outside from the towers. Such πύργοι 'towers' were above all to be found next to the gates, which we should imagine as provided with a projection jutting out far enough to give special protection to this important and most vulnerable part of the ring of fortifications.

This picture of the city fits very well with the fortifications of the first period which the excavations on Hissarlik have uncovered, where the circuit-walls show several tower extensions which jut out and the gates have massive projections; and it is consistent with all the passages of the poet in which πύργοι 'towers' are mentioned. Thus, to quote only a few, it is said in the *teichoscopia* of the old men of Troy Γ 149 εἴατο δημογέροντες ἐπὶ Σκαιῇσι πύλῃσιν 'the elders of the people were sitting at the Scaean gate', and immediately afterwards in the same sense it is said of them ἧντ᾽ ἐπὶ πύργῳ 'they were sitting on the tower', i.e. on the πύργος 'tower' which had been built for the protection of the Scaean Gate. In her anxiety Andromache too had hurried to this place when she had heard of the Trojans' difficulties. At Z 373 it is said of her: πύργῳ ἐφεστήκει γοόωσά τε μυρομένη τε 'she was standing on the tower weeping and lamenting', and likewise the housekeeper says about her: ἐπὶ πύργον ἔβη μέγαν Ἰλίου, οὕνεκ᾽ ἄκουσεν / τείρεσθαι Τρῶας 'She has gone to the great tower of Ilium, because she heard that our men were being ground down', and immediately afterwards, 388, generally indicating the direction she had taken: ἡ μὲν δὴ πρὸς τεῖχος ἐπειγομένη ἀφικάνει 'So she rushed out and must have arrived at the wall'; Hector then meets her, 392, εὖτε πύλας ἵκανε διερχόμενος μέγα ἄστυ / Σκαιάς, τῇ ἄρ᾽ ἔμελλε διεξίμεναι πεδίονδε 'when he had crossed the great town and reached the Scaean gate, his route out onto the plain'. At X 462 it is said of the same Andromache who had hurried out when she heard that Hector was alone outside the city, ἐπεὶ πύργον τε καὶ ἀνδρῶν ἷξεν ὅμιλον 'when she came to the tower where the men had gathered in a crowd'. So the crowd of men was to be found on the πύργος 'tower', and whoever came to the πύργος 'tower' reached the ὅμιλος ἀνδρῶν 'crowd of men' at the same time. But when she is looking around, searching for her Hector, she stood, 463, παπτήνασ᾽ ἐπὶ *τείχεϊ* 'looking along *the wall*', since now the notion of the length of the wall is coming to the fore. Corresponding to this notion of τεῖχος 'wall' it is said of Hector in flight from Achilles X 144 τρέσε δ᾽ Ἕκτωρ / *τεῖχος* ὕπο Τρώων 'Hector fled in terror under *the wall* of the Trojans', and 146 *τείχεος* αἰὲν ὑπὲκ καθ᾽ ἁμαξιτὸν ἐσσεύοντο 'always keeping some way from *the wall*, they sped along the waggon-track', but later, 194, ὁσσάκι δ᾽ ὁρμήσειε πυλάων Δαρδανιάων / ἀντίον ἀΐξασθαι, ἐϋδμήτους ὑπὸ πύργους, / εἴ πώς οἱ καθύπερθεν ἀλάλκοιεν βελέεσσιν, 'As often as Hector made a move towards the Dardanian gate, hoping to get close enough under the well-built towers for those above to protect him with their missiles'; for there **[II.21]** stood the Trojans watching the terrible spectacle. Hector X 35 stood προπάροιθε πυλάων 'in front of the gate', 97 *πύργῳ* ἔπι προύχοντι φαεινὴν ἀσπίδ᾽ ἐρείσας 'he leaned his glittering shield against the projecting *tower*' –

this is the projection of the Scaean Gate which was mentioned above, 112 it is said more generally in Hector's soliloquy εἰ ... ἀσπίδα ... καταθείομαι ... δόρυ δὲ πρὸς τεῖχος ἐρείσας 'If ... I put down ... my shield ... and prop my spear against the wall'. At Φ 526 Priam sees from the πύργος 'tower' the distress of the Trojans fleeing at speed to the city, ἑστήκει ... θείου ἐπὶ πύργου 'he stood on the divinely-built tower'; further it is said 529 οἰμώξας ἀπὸ πύργου βαῖνε χαμᾶζε 'he gave a cry of alarm and came down from the tower to the ground'; then he calls on the guards to open the gate, 530, ὀτρύνων παρὰ τεῖχος ... πυλαώρους 'giving urgent orders to the wall's gatekeepers', who therefore stood 'along the wall' next to the gates. As a consequence of the steep site of the city, Ἴλιος αἰπεινή 'steep Ilium', the towers were probably lower and easier to climb from the inside (as they were at Hissarlik), like the walls.

So these πύργοι 'towers' could take a considerable number of defenders, and from this one can also explain the meaning of the word πυργηδόν 'in a closed, tightly thronging crowd', used of the hunters M 43 who πυργηδὸν σφέας αὐτοὺς ἀρτύναντες 'closing their ranks, like a wall' face the lion, N 152 of the Greeks who thus try to fend off Hector who is charging at them, and O 618 likewise of the Greeks who are massed tightly together. In one passage, X 3, battlements on the wall also are mentioned. The Trojans who had fled into the city were κεκλιμένοι καλῇσιν ἐπάλξεσιν 'leaning against the fine battlements', whereas the Achaeans τείχεος ἆσσον ἴσαν σάκε' ὤμοισι κλίναντες 'advanced on the wall, their shields at the slope on their shoulders', so were advancing as if ready for an assault. The fact that they are mentioned only in this one passage and that we do not get to know all the defensive features in practical use is explained by the fact that, in all his battle descriptions, the poet does not or cannot present us with a single picture of a real assault on the city and the corresponding defence against such an assault. The discussion of a few passages can show us how the defence of a fortified city in the age of Homer was organised in other respects.

During the defence of their city, the poet has the Trojans supported by so many allies that supplying them with food causes Hector serious concern. We learn from Sarpedon's mouth what their task is when he confronts the fleeing Hector with the accusation of personal cowardice, Ŀ 471ff. 'You probably thought,' he says, 'that you could hold Troy without your own citizens and without your allies, just with your relations; but they all shirk battle because they are cowards; only we allies are fighting', 477, ἡμεῖς δ' αὖ μαχόμεσθ' οἵπερ τ' ἐπίκουροι ἔνειμεν 'while we do the fighting, who are here as your allies'. So Troy is defended by μάχεσθαι 'fighting', and in fact by fighting in the open field, for that is all Sarpedon speaks about. 'But you,' he continues, 'are standing there idle and do not even order the other Trojans to stand their ground and defend their wives', 486, μενέμεν καὶ ἀμυνέμεναι ὤρεσσιν. 'If you are beaten, 487-8, i.e. defeated in a field battle, then the Greeks will soon destroy your city as well.'

During their procession to appeal to Athene Z 305, the Trojan women plead: 'show yourself as the protectress of the city, ῥυσίπτολι, by breaking the spear of Diomedes and make him himself fall in front of the Scaean Gate', i.e. in the field of battle, since this is where Diomedes was just raging so terribly amongst the defenders of the city.

Z 431ff. Andromache begs Hector to preserve himself in the interests of her and her child, and with that aim – not to withdraw from the defence of his home city, that would have been an unworthy demand of the brave hero – but to defend the city from the wall (cf. Hentze, *Appendix*, with whose explanations of the necessity of verses 433-9 I completely agree). He should therefore draw up his men παρ' ἐρινεόν 'by the fig tree'. But the fig tree was on a hill in front of the city. So, even according to Andromache's wishes, the men are to take their position, not on the walls and behind the battlements of the fortress, but immediately in front of the city walls; they are just no longer **[II.22]** to be led by Hector into the plain to fight in the open field (cf. below on I 352). That this proposal of Andromache requires a return to the conduct of the war practised earlier is correctly pointed out by Kiene, whom Hentze quotes in the *Appendix*. But Hector's heroic honour does not allow him, 441-6, to restrict himself to merely leading the defence and to refrain from battle, αἴ κε κακὸς ὣς νόσφιν ἀλυσκάζω πολέμοιο 'if I hide myself like a coward from the fighting'. His whole nature requires him αἰεὶ καὶ πρώτοισι μετὰ Τρώεσσι μάχεσθαι 'always *to fight* in the front ranks of the Trojans', although he knows that one day Troy will fall whatever he does. So presumably the defence of the well-fortified city is theoretically possible without fighting in open field, but practically speaking the hero cannot act like that. The honour of a hero and a warrior demands that, when the enemy army draws itself up in front of the walls and offers battle, he goes into action against it and accepts battle. But what if this does not happen? Then the situation stays as it was in the first nine years. There is simply no fighting. The Greeks wait outside in their camp in front of the gates, and the Trojans in the city or under its walls. Hostile action is not used against the besieged, for example by severe pressure on their resolve through cutting off food or water, by direct attack against the city or by a bombardment. The besiegers are camped out in front of the city, feed themselves off the fruits of the land and behave like people who have all the time in the world to await the outcome. But the Trojans are forced to watch their once flourishing countryside now gradually being exhausted and resources in the city for the upkeep of foreign allies also becoming more and more scarce.

So the pressure must come from the besieged, to drive the enemy out of the land, and this is in fact how the course of the action takes shape in the period of the war presented to us by the poet. Everything depends on the Trojans succeeding in driving the foreigners out of their country, destroying their fortified camp and, if possible, through complete destruction of their ships making a repetition of the enemy invasion impossible. Thus the initiative is placed in the hands of the besieged. As long as they take no action, the besiegers too act, essentially, passively. If the city's inhabitants do not come out for battle, battle does not take place, and as long as the Trojans stayed only under the walls of their city, nothing happened on either side. The most important motive for this Trojan caution, according to the poet, is their fear of Achilles. Consequently he can demonstrate his bravery and superiority over the Trojans only in surprise attacks on individuals. Thus Achilles boasts I 352ff.: ὄφρα δ' ἐγὼ μετ' Ἀχαιοῖσιν πολέμιζον / οὐκ ἐθέλεσκε μάχην ἀπὸ τείχεος ὀρνύμεν Ἕκτωρ, / ἀλλ' ὅσον ἐς Σκαιάς τε πύλας καὶ φηγὸν ἵκανεν 'In the days when I took the field with the Greeks, Hector was not willing to start a fight away from the walls. He'd come no further than the Scaean gate and the oak-tree'. That this place lay outside the walls is shown by verse 355 in which Achilles says ἔνθα ποτ' οἶον ἔμιμνε 'once he did wait for me there on my own', i.e. to fight; but that it was situated very closely in front of the gates, i.e. presumably under the protection of the wall, follows from the fact that Hector Z 237-8 met the Trojan women there when he returned to Troy during the battle.

Hector himself calls his and his allies' activity ἀμφιμάχεσθαι 'fighting around', Z 460 Ἕκτορος ... ὃς ἀριστεύεσκε μάχεσθαι / Τρώων ἱπποδάμων, ὅτε Ἴλιον ἀμφεμάχοντο 'Hector ... who was the best of the horse-taming Trojans when they fought round Ilium', and Achilles too says of himself I 412 Τρώων πόλιν ἀμφιμάχωμαι 'I fight round the city of the Trojans'; but the war will only be finished when the Trojans have succeeded in forcing the Achaeans out of their country, Z 526 αἴ κέ ποθι Ζεὺς / δώῃ ... κρητῆρα στήσασθαι ἐλεύθερον ἐν μεγάροισιν / ἐκ Τροίης ἐλάσαντες ἐϋκνήμιδας Ἀχαιούς 'if Zeus ever lets us ... drive the well-greaved Achaeans from our soil and celebrate our freedom with drink-offerings in the palace.'

But the Achaeans will stay there and live off plundering the land until Troy capitulates, or they themselves are chased away – an 'either – or' which Hector also confirms when twice, by means of a duel based on an agreement made in advance, he makes the attempt to put an end to the endless fighting and waiting which has finally become more than both armies can bear, **[II.23]** H 71-2, εἰς ὅ κεν ἢ ὑμεῖς Τροίην εὔπυργον ἕλητε / ἢ αὐτοὶ παρὰ νηυσὶ δαμήετε ποντοπόροισιν 'till the day when you capture Troy with its fine towers, or succumb to us yourselves beside your seafaring ships'.

That the besiegers also are heartily fed up with the war is shown to us, apart from the great readiness with which Hector's proposal is received by the Greek army on both occasions, by a series of reactions illustrating the mood of the Greek army which the poet has skilfully woven into his account. But a decision by force can be brought about only by battle in the open field in front of the city. It is in this spirit that, when they want to make an end to the fighting on the first day of battle, Apollo says to Athene, H 29ff. νῦν μὲν παύσωμεν πόλεμον ... / σήμερον, ὕστερον αὖτε μαχήσοντ᾽, εἰς ὅ κε τέκμωρ / Ἰλίου εὕρωσιν, ἐπεὶ ὣς φίλον ἔπλετο θυμῷ / ὑμῖν ἀθανάτῃσι διαπραθέειν τόδε ἄστυ 'Let us end the fighting ... for today. They will fight again later, and go on till they reach their goal in Ilium, since you goddesses have set your hearts on razing this town to the ground.' Similarly, the impetuous Diomedes also wants to continue fighting on his own, naturally in the open field, with Sthenelus, even if all the Greeks depart, I 48-9 ἐγὼ Σθένελός τε μαχησόμεθ᾽, εἰς ὅ κε τέκμωρ / Ἰλίου εὕρωμεν. σὺν γὰρ θεῷ εἰλήλουθμεν 'We two, Sthenelus and I, will fight on till we reach our goal in Ilium. For we have come with divine support'. But how the city is to fall by this action we do not hear; even Diomedes himself does not know. Priam too says H 377 (396) 'let us first cremate the dead, ὕστερον αὖτε μαχησόμεθ᾽, εἰς ὅ κε δαίμων / ἄμμε διακρίνη 'We will fight again later, till the powers above decide between us'. The same attitude is the basis of verses Θ 55-8. It is the record of the beginning of the second day of fighting. The Greeks are arming for battle, the Trojans ἑτέρωθεν ἀνὰ πτόλιν ὡπλίζοντο / παυρότεροι, μέμασαν δὲ καὶ ὣς ὑσμῖνι μάχεσθαι, / χρειοῖ ἀναγκαίῃ, πρό τε παίδων καὶ πρὸ γυναικῶν 'were arming themselves in the town. There were fewer of them, yet they were still determined to *confront the enemy face-to-face*, driven as they were by the need to fight for their wives and children'. They would of course have found sufficient protection behind their walls, and no danger would have threatened their families there. But that would not have brought about a result, and it was in their interests to drive the enemy from their country and put an end to the war. How little they were restricted in their movements is clearly shown by verse 58: πᾶσαι δ᾽ ὠΐγνυντο πύλαι, ἐκ δ᾽ ἔσσυτο λαός 'The gates were all thrown open, and the army poured out'. So they could dare to do this without any apprehension, because the Achaeans never consider forcing their way through the open gates. Of course, against such a superior opponent as Achilles, battle in open field offered little prospect of success; and this is why, when the return of Achilles is imminent, Polydamas Σ 254ff. advises the Trojans to retire into the city while night allows them to make an undisturbed withdrawal, 267. Behind the walls the Trojans have nothing to fear, for, 274-6, ἄστυ δὲ πύργοι / ὑψηλαί τε πύλαι σανίδες τ' ἐπὶ τῆς ἀραρυῖαι / μακραὶ ἐΰξεστοι ἐζευγμέναι εἰρύσσονται 'the town will be safely protected by its walls, high gateways and great wooden doors fitted to them, firmly closed'. Next morning they should draw themselves up on the wall, ἂμ πύργους 'on the towers'; then Achilles will be in trouble if he wants to fight them for the city's possession; let him then drive his horses up and down all round in front of the city – actually below the city, since the plain is situated lower; he will hardly feel like forcing his way in, and will never destroy it if we limit ourselves to this type of defence behind the walls, Σ 279-83. Of course this proposal is unacceptable to the heroic Hector; he is tired of being shut up behind the walls; besides, the cost of providing food for the immense army has exhausted the rich resources of the city and the country; therefore a decision must be brought about in front of the walls 287-90. So the walls provide sufficient protection even against an attack by the most terrible opponent, Achilles, which is why Hecuba, too, X 84 begs Hector ἄμυνε δὲ δήϊον ἄνδρα / τείχεος ἐντὸς ἐών 'repel the enemy from inside the walls'. Of course Poseidon had built them, Φ 447, ἵν' ἄρρηκτος πόλις εἴη 'to make the town impregnable'. Accordingly, on the evening of the first day of battle, H 478ff., although threatening omens from Zeus fill the Trojans with anxious fear all night long, there is no mention of any measures they take for the protection of their city. It is merely said 480ff. οὐδέ τις ἔτλη / πρὶν πιέειν, πρὶν λεῖψαι ὑπερμενέϊ Κρονίωνι. / κοιμήσαντ' ἄρ' ἔπειτα καὶ ὕπνου δῶρον ἕλοντο 'Not a man dared to drink before he had made a libation to the almighty son of Cronus. Then they lay down and took the gift of sleep'.

In the evening of the second day of battle, Hector contents himself with issuing a proclamation that boys and old men **[II.24]** should defend the walls, Θ 518-19. This may not surprise us, since the entire Trojan army is camped out opposite the now defeated Greeks, from whom no vigorous attack was to be feared, but at most a surprise raid by a small force, 522 μὴ λόχος εἰσέλθῃσι πόλιν λαῶν ἀπεόντων 'so that no enemy raiding-party can steal into the town while the troops are away'. But the inhabitants of the besieged city on the shield of Achilles also leave the protection of their walls to the children and the old men, Σ 514ff., while they carry out an ambush on a herd of cattle being brought for slaughter to the besiegers, even though the situation appears more serious for them than for the Trojans. In this attack on the herds intended for the besieging troops, we hear of a new means of defence, whose execution shows us how little the poet understands the idea of a city besieged in our sense, i.e. encircled.

The extraordinary ease of contact between the besieged and the outside world, which it did not enter the minds of the besiegers to cut off,
is also proved by Priam's journey to the Greek camp. The king calmly
drives out of the city with his two vehicles, and relations and friends
accompany him out onto the plain, Ω 329-30. For Priam the danger
only begins when he enters the Greek camp, and for this part of his
journey the gods send him Hermes as the ideal protector.

Only to get a rich ransom did the besiegers lie in wait to capture
individual eminent Trojans, as Achilles did Lycaon Φ 35ff. τόν ῥά ποτ'
αὐτὸς / ἦγε λαβών 'whom once before he had taken captive'. This is why
Priam Ω 778 says to the Trojans, whom he calls on to gather wood for
burning Hector's corpse during the truce agreed with Achilles, ... μηδέ
τι θυμῷ / δείσητ' Ἀργείων πυκινὸν λόχον 'do not be afraid of a Greek
ambush'. There is no thought at all of any measures the Greeks might
take, e.g. to prevent supplies being brought into Troy at this time; the
eleven-day truce for Hector's funeral celebrations is granted without
any limitation, Ω 664ff. But even after the death of Troy's bravest
defender, the strong walls retain their impregnable resistance until
cunning and treachery hand the colossal fortress over to the besieging
army. Courage and bravery had not been able to achieve this end;
even to Achilles, the epitome of these qualities, this finest fruit of his
ruthless daring was not given.

We still have to mention briefly one more solution capable of bringing about a decision between the two warring parties without blood-
shed. It consisted in the besieged people paying for the withdrawal of
the enemy army by a heavy fine. Given the modest knowledge of the
art of siege and the impossibility, even with a superior army, of forcing a well-fortified city to surrender, this solution was perhaps used
quite often. For the besieged city on the shield of Achilles, the division
of all their possessions is mentioned as the price of ransom, Σ 510-11
δίχα δέ σφισιν ἥνδανε βουλή, / ἠὲ διαπραθέειν ἢ ἄνδιχα πάντα δάσασθαι
'The besiegers were in two minds, whether to sack the place outright,
or to take half the possessions'. And Hector too, before his duel with
Achilles, seriously considers whether he should not try to buy peace
and the withdrawal of the Greeks by an equal division of possessions,
Χ 119-20 Τρωσὶν ... γερούσιον ὅρκον ἕλωμαι / μή τι κατακρύψειν, ἀλλ'
ἄνδιχα πάντα δάσασθαι 'and on behalf of the Trojans ... I take an oath
with the elders in council not to hide anything but to divide it all up
equally'. Half of one's possessions may have been a usual settlement,
but no doubt the heaviness of the price depended on the greater or
lesser pressure under which the besieged found themselves.

We must here break off our reflections on battle and its description
in Homer. However incomplete they may be in many respects, they
have still shown us that battle in the open field already depends on

numerous tactical skills, that the security measures taken by besieging troops in posting guards and **[II.25]** sheltering themselves in a camp fortified with wall and ditch point to no little experience, but that we cannot yet speak of any art of siege or of attack against a fortified city. There is not even a trace of the extension of the wall which the besiegers build for their own protection to a circumvallation around the city, which might reasonably suggest itself. The besieging army is almost powerless in the face of a city encircled by walls, and this situation remains largely unchanged until a new period of siege-warfare begins with the older Dionysius.[10] Cf. H. Droysen, *Heerwesen und Kriegführung der Griechen*, p. 207ff.

Notes

1. Cf. n. 2 on p. 91.

2. 'Ajax' on its own usually means the son of Telamon, but here there are strong reasons for supposing the reference is to the son of Oileus.

3. This analytical criticism, derived from Ameis-Hentze, has been repeated by many later commentators. In fact, the poet reports the separate attacks of the third, fifth and first divisions, and should not be expected to give a prosaic report of what happened to all five.

4. Hagen von Tronje and Volker von Alzei are Burgundian heroes in the *Nibelungenlied*, who take up a position together in front of Kriemhild's palace in the land of the Huns.

5. See line 381.

6. More precisely, Hentze, *Appendix* to N, Intro. p. 22.

7. Not to speak of Odysseus, B 278.

8. In the British Museum, London. Illustrated on p. N 10 of K. Fittschen's *Der Schild des Achilleus* (*Archaeologia Homerica, Bildkunst, Teil 1*), as well as by Helbig (op. cit.), and on p. 205 of *The Iliad: A Commentary*, vol. V, ed. M.W. Edwards, Cambridge 1991.

9. Heinrich Schliemann excavated on the site of Hissarlik, identified as Troy, between 1870 and 1890, publishing his results at intervals. The 'first period', mentioned by Albracht, with massive fortification walls, was later shown to have been before 2000 BC, long before the date of Priam's Troy; the Troy which would suit the assumed date of the Trojan War (about 1200 BC) is one or other of the archaeological levels defined as Troy VI or VIIa.

10. Dionysius I, tyrant of Syracuse from 405 to 367, learnt new siege techniques from his enemies the Carthaginians in Sicily, including close investment of the besieged city and the use of catapults against the walls. His methods were taken over by the successful generals of the following period, Philip and Alexander of Macedon.

Bibliography

Ameis = *Homers Ilias, für den Schulgebrauch erklärt von K.F. Ameis und C. Hentze*; 1st ed., Leipzig 1868-84.

Ameis-Hentze: see Ameis.

Buchholz, E.A.W., *Die homerische Realien*, 3 vols, Leipzig 1871-5.

Droysen, H., *Heerwesen und Kriegführung der Griechen*, Freiburg i. B., 1888.

Duncker, M.W., *Geschichte des Altertums*, 4 vols, 1st ed., Berlin 1852-7.

Düntzer, H., *Homers Ilias. Erklärende Schulausgabe*, 2nd ed., Paderborn 1873-8.

Faesi = *Homers Iliade*, erklärt von J.U. Faesi, 2 vols, Leipzig 1851-2.

Faesi-Franke = *Homers Iliade*, erklärt von J.U. Faesi, Sechste Auflage, besorgt von F.R. Franke, 4 vols, Berlin, Leipzig, Altenburg 1877-80.

Franke: see Faesi-Franke.

Friedreich, J.B., *Die Realien in der Iliade und Odyssee*, 2nd ed., Erlangen 1856.

Frölich, H., *Die Militärmedicin Homer's*, Stuttgart 1879.

Helbig, W.H., *Das homerische Epos aus den Denkmälern erläutert*, 1st ed., Leipzig 1884, 2nd ed., Leipzig 1887.

Hentze = *Anhang [Appendix] zu Homers Ilias, Schulausgabe von K.F. Ameis und C. Hentze*, 1st ed., Leipzig 1870-86.

Hopf, J., *Das Kriegswesen im heroischen Zeitalter nach Homer*, Gymn.-Progr. 4, Hamm, 1847, 1858.

Jähns, M., *Die Entwickelung des altgriechischen Kriegswesens*, Grenzboten 1878.

Kiene, A., *Die Komposition der Ilias des Homer*, Göttingen 1864.

Köchly und Rüstow = F.W. Rüstow and H.A.T. Köchly, *Geschichte des griechischen Kriegswesens, von der altesten Zeit bis auf Pyrrhos*, Aarau 1852.

Köpke, G.G.S., *Über das Kriegswesen der Griechen im heroischen Zeitalter*, Berlin 1807.

La Roche, J., *Homerische Studien. Der Accusativ im Homer*, Vienna, 1861.

La Roche, J., *Homers Ilias, für den Schulgebrauch erklärt*, 6 parts, Berlin 1870-1.

Lexicon Homericum, ed. H.E. Ebeling [the contributors include F. Albracht (see p. 48) and B. Giseke (see p. 68)], Leipzig 1871-85.

Menge, R., *Troia und die Troas*, 1st ed., Gütersloh 1891.

Passow, F.L.C.F., *Handwörterbuch der griechischen Sprache*, (begrundet von Franz Passow, neu bearbeitet von V.C.F. Rost und F. Palm), 5th ed., 2 Bande (in 4), Leipzig 1841-57.

Ribbeck, W., in *Neue Jahrbücher für Philologie und Paedagogik*, vol. 85 (1862), p. 89 (in a review of A. Köchly, *Iliadis Carmina XVI*, Leipzig 1861).

Rüstow, F.W., *Heerwesen und Kriegsführung C.J. Cäsars*, 1st ed., Gotha 1855.

Sainte-Beuve, C.A., 'Le premier livre de l'Énéide', in *Revue Contemporaine* (first series), XXVIII, Paris 1856.

Index Locorum

Appendix

Malcolm Willcock

In more than a century since Albracht wrote, relatively little attention has been paid to the battle scenes. Although fighting takes up about a third of the narrative of the *Iliad*, and was evidently fascinating to the poet and his ancient audience, it has been largely disregarded by the moderns. The reasons may have included a distaste for descriptions of fighting and killing or a mistaken perception that the battle scenes are monotonous. In any case, other issues occupied the minds of Homeric scholars, especially the long dispute between Analysts and Unitarians, and later the emergence of 'oral theory' in America, diverging from the German and European traditions. Also Albracht's work had appeared in the Annual Reports of his schools, and, though relatively easily available in Germany, was less accessible elsewhere.

The great period of German scholarly devotion to the *Iliad*, dominated eventually by Wilamowitz and Schadewaldt, carried on at least until the 1930s and the Second World War. After the war there was some loosening of constraints and broadening of approach. In 1954 appeared an excellent doctoral thesis by Gisela Strasburger about the minor figures in the battle scenes. In 1968, the American scholar Bernard Fenik applied the oral approach to this aspect of the epic in *Typical Battle Scenes in the Iliad*. Neither Strasburger nor Fenik, however, is influenced by Albracht. The former is concerned with the poet's interest in individuals, not the descriptions of fighting; the latter with repetition of situation in the light of oral theory, treating the incidents which are described as deriving from the technique of the bard, not as a reflection of any kind of activity in the real world.

A major contribution appeared in 1977 with *Kampfparänese, Kampfdarstellung und Kampfwirklichkeit in der Ilias, bei Kallinos und Tyrtaios* by Joachim Latacz. One of Latacz's most persuasive points was that the *Iliad*, while cataloguing the achievements of the leading fighters on both sides, does not lose sight of the involvement of the whole armies. He produced a schematisation of the Homeric battle, not in fact very different from Albracht's, claiming that it begins with a stand-off, which he calls the 'Massenwurfkampf' ('massed missile fighting', what Albracht calls the 'standing fight') in which the armies are drawn up facing each other at a short distance and exchanging fire, as it were; from it develops what he calls the 'Promachoi-Kampf' in which individual warriors move forward from their own line to engage the enemy either in general or targeting a particular opponent; then the armies close, the 'promachoi' move back into their own lines, and a massed engagement develops (called by Latacz a 'Massennahkampf', i.e. hand-to-hand fighting). This leads eventually to one battle-line breaking and a rout, in which chariots are used on both sides. When the defeated rally, the battle begins again, with 'Massenwurfkampf' and 'Promachoi-Kampf'.

About that time in the history of discussion a renewed interest in the Homeric battles was being shown by ancient historians, concerned particularly with the early development of the heavily armed hoplite phalanx, which dominated the wars between Greek cities for several hundred years. Their interest was in whether the *Iliad* ever reflects the beginnings of hoplite warfare, for example in some striking descriptions of very close formations (12.105, 13.130-5, 16.214-7). This raises also the general question considered by Albracht, whether Homer's descriptions are based on the fighting methods of his day and thus to an extent historical, or whether they depend rather on poetical tradition and invention.

An original and somewhat eccentric approach began in 1986 in a number of relatively short articles and contributions by the Dutch scholar Hans van Wees, himself an ancient historian rather than a Homerist. He draws very different conclusions from Albracht and Latacz, seeing the situation on the battlefield as much more fluid and less schematised than they, closer indeed (in a striking parallel) to running fights between football supporters or between rioters and the police; for him *promachoi*, far from being individuals who had stepped forward from the front line of their army, constituted rather all those who were engaged with the enemy at any given time; another repeated argument of his is that the actions ascribed to the major heroes are not to be thought of as individual exploits, but that each was understood to be accompanied by his own men, even Odysseus and Diomedes in 11 (cf. Albracht p. 75 on the Greeks who took part in the rearguard action organised by Thoas at 15.281ff.).

Most recently O. Hellmann summarises the present state of scholarship on the subject, covering all aspects with sound and balanced judgement. Perhaps his most important contribution lies in his understanding that the descriptions of fighting do not aim for historical accuracy, but rather serve the poet's purpose to describe a world of heroic individuals.

Appendix

There are four basic questions:

The 'standing fight'

This is the one area in which modern scholarship firmly disagrees with Albracht. He takes the term σταδίη μάχη[1] 'standing fight' to refer to what he sees as the commonest battle situation, when the armies stand in line facing each other at a short distance (thirty to forty paces at the most, p. 32) and exchanging missiles, what Latacz calls the 'Massenwurfkampf'. But the evidence of the text is that σταδίη on the contrary refers to hand-to-hand close fighting and is actually contrasted with the use of missiles such as arrows or javelins (see 13.314, 713, 15.282-3). It is when the battle is *stationary* (σταδίη), the armies are locked together and neither gives way, in fact the alternative to rout. So Latacz 68 n. 2, van Wees (1996) 3, Hellmann 140-1. Indeed there is serious doubt whether 'Massenwurfkampf' is a stage in the battle at all; certainly in the first engagement, which acts as a paradigm for the rest, the armies clash immediately, without any preliminary stand-off (4.446-56).

The promachoi ('front fighters')

The interpretation is confused. Albracht and Latacz sometimes assume that these are the front line of the contingents, sometimes the warriors who step out of the front line to engage the enemy; Van Wees argues that they are all those who are currently fighting; Hellmann that they are the leaders and best fighters, often operating independently of the front line of the army. This seems correct; the word certainly means 'those who fight in front'.

The hoplite phalanx

Few now see a direct allusion to heavily armed hoplite fighting even in the few descriptions of very tight formations. Latacz and van Wees argue convincingly against it, and see also Snodgrass. For this reason we have decided not to follow Homer and Albracht in using the term 'phalanx' for the closed ranks of the armies, as it would risk giving the wrong impression.

Homer's detailed presentation

Commentators have struggled with the implications of Homer's practice of describing the events on the battlefield as a succession of actions by named heroes, not for the most part duels, but successes of individuals in the killing of named opponents. Albracht seems to have the right idea here, that they represent the course of the battle, in his

---

1. The term is doubtful, for it is not found as such in the *Iliad*, which uses σταδίη ὑσμίνη or just σταδίη; αὐτοσταδίη is found once (13.325).

repeated observation that in a rout only soldiers of the defeated army are listed as casualties. Strasburger 47-8 speaks of *Konkretisierung*, presumably meaning by this the provision of corroborative detail to strengthen and confirm the narrative. Latacz 76-8, 225, says that the killings described are *examples* of what is happening all along the battle-line. But they are surely not simply examples, for these highlighted victors are the great heroic fighters, not a selection from a larger number. They certainly represent the way the battle is going, but they also have the artistic (and unhistorical) effect of concentrating the narrative on the achievements of the major heroes and the pathos of their victims. Hellmann 166-9 describes them as not so much 'exemplary' as 'epideictic' (demonstrative), and not so much realistic as poetic.

The issues Albracht so perceptively discussed have thus eventually been considered further by scholars, or at least those in the first part of his work, related to the fighting on the plain. His other excellences, especially those in Part II, about the possibilities of attack on fortified camps and walled cities, remain as fresh as when he first wrote them.

Bibliography

Fenik, B., *Typical Battle Scenes in the Iliad* (Hermes Einzelschriften 21), Wiesbaden 1968.

Hellmann, O., *Die Schlachtszenen der Ilias* (Hermes Einzelschriften 83), Stuttgart 2000.

Latacz, J., *Kampfparänese, Kampfdarstellung und Kampfwirklichkeit in der Ilias, bei Kallinos und Tyrtaios* (Zetemata 66), Munich 1977.

Snodgrass, A.M., 'The "Hoplite Reform" revisited', *Dialogues d'histoire ancienne*, 19 (1993) 47-61.

Strasburger, G., *Die kleinen Kämpfer der Ilias*, Frankfurt 1954.

van Wees, H., 'Leaders of men? Military organisation in the Iliad', *CQ* 36 (1986) 285-303.

———— 'Kings in combat. Battles and heroes in the Iliad', *CQ* 38 (1988) 1-24.

———— 'Heroes, knights and nutters', in *Battle in Antiquity*, ed. A.B. Lloyd, London 1996, pp. 1-86.

———— 'Homeric warfare', in *A New Companion to Homer*, ed. I. Morris and B. Powell, Leiden 1997, pp. 668-93.

Willcock, M.M., 'The Fighting in the Iliad', in ΣΠΟΝΔΕΣ ΣΤΟΝ ΟΜΗΡΟ (Proceedings of the Sixth Congress arranged by the Centre for Odyssean Studies, September 1990. In memory of J.T. Kakridis), ed. M. Païzi-Apostolopoulou, Ithaka 1993, pp. 141-7.